GW00870151

PHANTASMAGORIA MAGAZINE

Issue 5, summer 2018

CONTENTS

Waring

Editors: Trevor Kennedy and Allison Weir

Consultant Editor: John Gilbert

Supporting Editors: Helen Scott and Nancy Chandler

Cover artwork and design: Joe Harris

Contributors: Richard Barr, Abdul-Qaadir Taariq Bakari-Muhammad, Andrea Bickerstaff, David Brilliance, Stephen Clarke, Kellie-Ann Bernadette Crawford, Christina Engela, Carl R. Jennings, Owen Quinn, Karina Sims, David A. Sutton and Nathan Waring.

Published by Phantasmagoria Publishing through CreateSpace

EDITORIAL

Evolution

Phantasmagoria Magazine is evolving, growing in spectacular ways. We are now receiving the right kind of attention from some of the biggest names in UK horror/weird fiction and further afield. In addition, we have now landed in certain shops, including the Belfast City Centre branch of Forbidden Planet (thank you, Mal!) and even my local Vivo, also Belfast-based and located on 937 Crumlin Road (thanks to Michael for this!). We fully intend for this to be just the beginning of our 1980s-esque genre magazine revival and the world (and its shops) is our oyster! According to my contact at Forbidden Planet, Malachi, there is a real hunger for our specific brand of publication and that can therefore only mean good news for our hard working team here and, of course, you, the reader.

It must be said though, that an interest in our type of magazine is all good and well, but we must never allow ourselves the luxury of resting on our laurels and taking our collective feet off the accelerator pedal. We must continue to grow, relentlessly pumping out material of a high quality. Anything less would be a gross injustice to ourselves and the readership and simply will not suffice. That's not to say we don't enjoy what we do here. We love it, if truth be told! And for myself personally, it is a bit of a childhood dream realised and beyond. I foresee a bright future for Phantasmagoria Magazine, but the hard, time-consuming work must not be underestimated either.

In this current bumper edition we have a chat with horror author/*Star Wars* actor/80s pop star/photographer (is there anything he can't do?!), Tim Dry. We also speak to Polish dark poet, Norbert Gora, who has also been kind enough to allow us the privilege of a peek at some of his unpublished work.

Our big features for this issue are also of a diverse and highly interesting nature. John Gilbert takes a look at the life and legacy of JRR Tolkien, especially of interest with a new big budget *The Lord of the Rings* television series now in the works. David Sutton takes us on a journey to Victorian Ireland to meet the great ghost story writer, Joseph Sheridan Le Fanu, whilst newcomer, Nathan Waring, gets to grips with the history of Kaiju cinema and the king of the monsters himself, Godzilla. Not forgetting Owen Quinn's tribute to screen legend Peter Cushing and to top all this off, team regular David Brilliance gives his valued opinion on the BBC 1990s horror film double bill revival which was presented by the formidable Dr. Terror.

As if all this wasn't enough, we also have our regular reviews section and original fiction from the aforementioned John Gilbert, South African author, Christina Engela, Canadian wordsmith, Karina Sims, and local lad, Richard Barr.

I know, I know, we're spoiling you again, haha!

So until next time, have an amazing summer and we'll see you again at the end of August, where we will have a couple of big surprises in store. Watch this space!

Trevor Kennedy,
Belfast,
June 2018.

After his great success in saving the last remaining Knucker Dragon from being hunted and killed, young Drefan is desperate to set out on a new adventure. His great friend, Kendra, an old Wicce who lives near his home, thrills him with her tales of the strange and wonderful creatures which inhabit the great Wildwood, and the eleven year old Drefan is determined to try and find for himself some of those beings of which she has spoken.

But the Wildwood is not a safe place to visit in the Englaland of the year 550. Terrible shape-shifting beasts haunt the dark woods, packs of Grey Wolves and wild boar with their huge slashing tusks roam freely, and only the Gods knew what else lurked within...

Available to purchase from Amazon

DRY WIT

Trevor Kennedy chats to a man with a highly impressive CV - horror author, 1980s pop star, photographer and *Star Wars* actor, **Tim Dry**.

TK: Tim, it's a real coup for us here at *Phantasmagoria Magazine* to chat with someone with such an impressive and varied back catalogue of creative work as yourself. Back in the 1980s (a glorious decade for many reasons, by the way!), you were one half of Tik and Tok, a duo that combined mime, robotics and electronic synthesizer-based music (which I still love). You performed with some of the biggest pop acts of the time, including Duran Duran, Gary Numan, Depeche Mode, Ultravox and many more. It must have been quite an amazing time for you. Could you tell us a bit more about it please, including what it was like to perform in front of none other than Queen Elizabeth II herself?

Tim Dry: Way back in 1979, I was working with my then partner, Barbie Wilde (later to be an actress in *Hellbound*: *Hellraiser II* and in the 2000s the author of *The Venus Complex* and *Voices Of The Damned*) in our own duo mime show called *Drawing In Space*. We were silent and white-faced and pretty traditional. We were performing in Fringe theatres and other small venues in and around London to small but appreciative audiences but we wanted more! We wanted loud music! Lights! Colour and action!

Suddenly we became involved with a frenetic and talented man named Robert Pereno who asked us to join a dance group he had named Shock. We did and there we were - two mime artists now working with three dancers. One day we met a pretty young lad named Sean in the pub after a mime class. We got chatting and he told us that he'd got a solo act called Plastic Joe that involved him dressing all in black plastic with melting face make up and standing totally motionless on the street and terrifying passers by when he swung into robotic action. We told him that he had to join our group Shock and he did. So now we were three mimes and three dancers and it was a good balance. We got drawn into the whole New Romantic/Blitz Club scene in London through Rusty Egan (drummer in Visage) and Richard Burgess (drummer in Landscape) and we became very popular and got a lot of press. We recorded two dance floor classic singles and we supported Gary Numan, Ultravox, Depeche Mode and several others as the whole music and fashion scene shifted from grey to technicolour almost overnight. It was very exciting to be right in the centre of the cyclone as it began to change the shapes

9

and sounds of English music and fashion. We knew and hung out with Duran Duran, Spandau Ballet, Soft Cell, Adam Ant and all the other new bands.

One night, in a break from Shock's frenetic gig and press activities in July 1980, Sean and I decided to go busking as robots in full evening dress with white face, shades and white gloves. We stood outside a posh restaurant in Knightsbridge, London and every time anyone came in or out of the restaurant we'd glide towards them as mechanical people and it used to freak them right out! So much so that they threw pound notes into the top hat we'd placed in front of us. We thought that this was a really cool thing to do to make money so we did it again the next night and the night after that as we were making more cash than we were in Shock. Sean said we should name ourselves 'Tik & Tok' and my contribution to that was saying that we should spell it with a 'K' not a 'C' or a 'CK'. The name was an inspired idea as it suggested mechanical movement and it also rhymed with Shock. Tik & Tok became a full blown entity in their own right after Shock split up in 1981 and then we started to make our own music and record and release singles.

Tik & Tok were invited to support Gary Numan on his 'Comeback' tour *Warriors* in 1983 as we'd become friends with him after Shock supported him during his farewell shows at Wembley Arena in April 1981. It was a seven week tour of the UK that took in pretty much every major city and I have to say that for me it was the most exciting time of my life at that point. Every night as T&T we would do our act in front of an average of three thousand people and they all loved us! Very unusual for a support act, believe me! Our second single got into the Top 70 because of that. Towards the end of the tour we were contacted by the producers of The Royal Variety Performance 1983 to participate in the show for about a minute doing our robot act live in front of not only HRH The Queen, Sir Laurence Olivier but also approximately fourteen million people at home watching us on TV! It doesn't really get any bigger than that! Very exciting but at the same time somewhat terrifying.

TK: One of my earliest and happiest memories is of being brought to see *Star Wars: Return of the Jedi* with my father, uncle, cousins and best friend. I was seven years old at the time and still to this day the first act of that film - concerning that evil, giant, talking gangster slug, Jabba the Hutt, and set in and around his palace and sail barge - rank as some my favourite Star Wars moments (and I've seen all the films!). You appeared in those two segments of the film as one of Jabba the Hutt's henchmen, but also later on as a Mon Calamari Officer on Admiral Ackbar's ship. What was it like to act in one of the most iconic film series of all time? Do you still get asked for autographs and to appear at conventions? And what was Jabba himself like to work alongside?

Tim Dry: What can I say? It was then and still is to this very day the most exciting, awe-inspiring and magical job as a performer that I've ever done! Sean and I and about twenty other mime artistes auditioned in front of our tutor Desmond Jones and the producer of 'Jedi', Robert Watts, at Desmond's mime school in early January 1982. He told us that they were looking for mimes to play alien creatures in the new *Star Wars* movie. We did some weird kind of 'Alien Acting' and then went home. We both absolutely loved the first two movies and thought how utterly cool it would be to maybe actually be in the next one. We carried on doing Tik & Tok stuff until Desmond rang about a week later and said that we'd got the job! I was to play Tooth Face and Sean was to play Yak Face. Later on, many years later we discovered that we had grown character names – 'J'Quille' and 'Saelt Marae'. But flashing back now to January 1982.

The first day on set (after having spent a couple of days in wardrobe fittings etc) was totally mind-blowing! Everything was absolutely real! Four slimy and grubby walls in Jabba's palace plus a ceiling and floor and alcoves too. We were six feet off the ground because they had to have room for puppeteers to work and our costumes and creature heads were enormously hot, heavy and uncomfortable. There were all of us alien creatures plus extras, camera crews, make up and costume people, plus the cameras, director, assistant directors, lights, smoke machines etc in a fairly confined space. It was Hell I tell ya! But we survived and we were well paid and we got to hang out with Mark Hamill in downtime and made passing contact with Carrie and Harrison. It was three weeks as Jabba's boys and then we got the call to try on costumes for Mon Calamari Officers. They fitted and so we got that job too! They were a joy to wear after enduring three weeks of the heavy and stinky 'Jabba's Pal's' outfits.

To this very day Sean and I (and a whole host of other *Star Wars* performers) get invited to and sign autographs at conventions all over the world. Never in a million years could we have imagined back in 1982, that all this time later this would continue to be happening. It's wonderful and I love every moment of doing autograph shows. Thank you, Mr Lucas!

(Pictures copyright of Lucasfilm/Twentieth Century Fox).

TK: You have also appeared in other cult films and television shows, such as *Xtro* (1982), *Death Wish 3* (1985), *The Kenny Everett Show* and *Father Ted*. What were Charles Bronson and Kenny Everett like to work with? Was Kenny as insane in real life as he was in his act? Growing up, I was a fan of him and the *Death Wish* films, not to mention *Father Ted* too, of course.

Tim Dry: Unfortunately I never met Charles Bronson on the set of *Death Wish III*. I was just one of many angry punks with bad hair running around clutching a handgun whilst he was safe in his trailer! Kenny Everett was in reality a somewhat quiet and thoughtful professional in rehearsals and he learned his lines and knew his marks. As soon as the cameras rolled however the extrovert Kenny came into play and that was fantastic to see! The cast of *Father Ted* were all very friendly and welcoming even though I was only a guest artiste for the episode 'Kicking Bishop Brennan Up the Arse'! It's very 'out there' comedy and still retains its quirky charm to this day.

TK: You are now a horror author, contributing stories to some very well respected anthology series' and in addition you have recently published a new novella, *Ricochet*. Could you tell the readers and myself what *Ricochet* is all about please?

Tim Dry: My tagline for my novella *Ricochet* is: 'Reality is just a fragment of your imagination'. It's an attempt to dispel the notion that a story doesn't always have to follow the conventional narrative arc of taking the reader from a linear beginning at A and ending conclusively at Z. I don't personally believe that our minds are always so conservatively restrained by that notion. Are our dreams rational? Logical? Linear? Well for me they are most definitely not. They are a random collision of past, present and future in no definable order. I have a sneaking suspicion that there has always been a lot more going on in our subconscious minds than we have been coerced into believing. The work of film directors like Nicolas Roeg, Terry Gilliam and Jodorowski for example and writers like Colin Wilson, Burroughs, Hunter S. Thompson, Michael Moorcock and J. W. Dunne dispel the myth that time is linear and thus conventional. *Ricochet* for me was the long-awaited chance to somehow conjure that notion into a literary form, shake the dice and see where they land in the belief that everything actually IS somehow connected whether we're aware of it consciously or not. Putting that aside I wanted to entertain, delight, frighten, disgust and intrigue anyone who reads it. It's a graphic novel without any pictures. I'll leave those up to you!

TK: What attracts you to the horror genre and what do you believe makes a good horror story?

Tim Dry: I don't believe that I am actually a 'horror writer'. I see myself more as being a conduit for expressing dark and/or speculative fiction. The whole 'horror' genre for me is, with a few exceptions, apparently content to be reliant upon the same old clichés and jump scares. You know the stuff – Lovecraftian beings issuing forth and laying waste to townships, vampires both aged and young and sparkly, rising from graves to seek their prey, masked and badly-dressed sociopaths armed with chainsaws or rusty and crusted blades or machetes hacking up squealing teenagers, malevolent clowns, soiled beings brought back from the dead to wreak terrible revenge etc, etc.

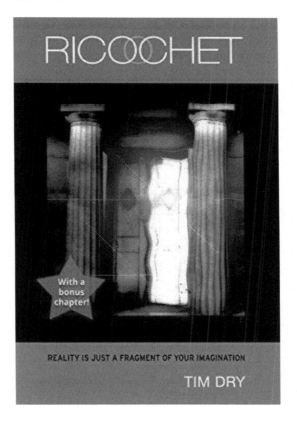

For me a good horror story is the one that delves into the mind and motivations of those who do a 'bad thing' just because they guiltlessly can. There will always be blood, retribution and subsequent punishment but I always want to know why and how.

Stephen King's intuitive grasp of character in nearly all of his novels is what inspires me. For example, the most terrifying elements of *The Shining* are not the body in the bathtub in Room 237 or the apparitions in the ballroom and the spectral bartender but the fact that here is a recovering alcoholic with writers block and enormous guilt because he damaged his only child trapped for the whole winter in an isolated hotel. To me that's horrific. It can only end badly. What King does so cleverly is to then weave in a supernatural entity which is the hotel itself and thus it eats away at Jack Torrance and his troubled soul. That's a double whammy but it's the damaged Jack that is the real horror in this story. That's what excites me.

TK: You are also a well-respected and successful photographer, photographing the likes of Mick Jagger, Joan Collins and more, and having your work appear in The National Portrait Gallery and other international galleries in London, New York, Berlin and Hamburg. How did you get into this type of work and is there anyone out there whom you would still like to photograph?

Tim Dry: I trained initially as a Graphic Designer at Art School in the early 1970s. I learnt some basics but I realised that I'd made a wrong choice after a couple of years (I should have studied Fine Art) and so I left to become a hippie living in Brighton by the sea and taking any drug that came my way and exploring inner space through the written word and the language of music. Eventually I resurfaced back on planet Earth and went off to London to study mime and enjoy all that resulted from it. Sometime around 1990 an old friend of mine showed me a Pentax SLR camera that he had just bought and I thought I would treat myself to one. I did and so I began to learn the basics of the art of not only taking photographs but also developing them in your own darkroom at home. An obsession was born! I pretty much forsook everything else (except for appearing in well-paid TV Commercials) to pursue this wondrous and magical art form that I actually had complete control over. I started to actually sell my work (sporadically). I was happy! I would have loved to photograph the late David Bowie in any of his guises. Kate Bush too.

TK: Which of your many mastered art forms do you prefer - music, acting, writing or photography?

Tim Dry: All of them! At any time, anywhere!

TK: Have you ever tried your hand at any other creative roles, directing for example?

Tim Dry: No, to be honest. Although I have on occasion thought about directing but it would have to be (if it ever happened) film and not theatre. But on a lighter note -I tried to master the ancient discipline of Cat Juggling a few years back but it ended quite badly with some fairly severe blood loss from exposed fleshy extremities, so I ditched it. Cats huh?

TK: So what do you have lined up next then, Tim, in what I can only presume is a very busy schedule of yours?

Tim Dry: I feel that moulding unholy creatures in all shapes and sizes in flesh-coloured plasticine is now my only true vocation. It's a long and sometimes lonely job I admit but as long as there are people out there who love me I know that my new work is SO worthwhile! Seriously? I have more short stories to write and quite possibly a new novella too. I have a major writing project in mind for the future but I'm not going to talk about that! I'll continue to be an autograph guest at conventions worldwide and maybe I'll make some more music at some point. I'm currently taking a great many photographs of London as I love the city and want to show the good bits to people.

TK: Tim, it has been truly fascinating speaking to you and we look forward to hearing about your future work, which I'm sure will be as well received as always.

(You can check out our review of Tim Dry's *Ricochet* in the reviews section).

TOLKIEN: ORIGINS OF MIDDLE-EARTH

On the opening of a major exhibition at Oxford's Bodleian Library, **John Gilbert** examines the rich and powerful literary legacy of **JRR Tolkien**.

Some say that Middle-earth exists. For the thousands of readers who visit or revisit its forests, rolling landscapes and ancient cities every year in their imaginations, that may be true. Middle-earth comprises an immersive landscape full of authentic cultures and characters, a terrain that echoes with heroic and bloody deeds; it has inspired many authors in the decades since it was published to pen their own fantastical tales. For some it is the font of the fantasy genre they love so much while for others it is a work of literature that forms the bedrock of their lives. It is not a book to be read just once, for the call of *The Lord of The Rings* seduces readers back between its pages again and again.

That just one man is responsible for such a behemoth of fantastical creativity would have been miraculous if that man had not been of the stature of JRR Tolkien. Born in South Africa in 1892 of middle class parents - his father was a bank manager - few could have guessed that, by the age of six, John Ronald Reuel Tolkien would have developed a fascination with 'made up' languages that was to take him to the academic towers of Oxford, and beyond to literary giant-hood.

Tolkien's childhood was, however, blighted by tragedy. At the age of three, whilst on a return trip with his mother to England, he learned that his father had died of Rheumatic Fever. Resulting financial hardship drove his mother to move the family in with her parents in Kings Heath, Birmingham, until in 1896 they moved to Sarehole - now Hall Green - which was then in Worcestershire but was later incorporated within the boundaries of an expanding Birmingham.

Ronald, as many of his friends called him, soon got the bug for exploring the local landmarks such as the Malvern, Clent and Lickey Hills, Moseley Bog and Sarehole Mill. These evocative locations would soon form the basis of scenes in his books. Indeed, his aunt Jane's farm, Bag End, was soon to give a home to a rather famous family of Hobbits.

Tolkien's mother, Mabel, educated Ronald and his younger

brother, Hilary, at home. He soon became interested in particular in Botany, in the life-cycles, the look and feel of plants which led to take up drawing in the great outdoors. It was, however, languages which drew his particular interest. He could read by the age of four and write by the time he was six. By the age of seven he had even mastered the rudiments of Latin. It was not, however, to the likes of *Treasure Island* or *Alice In Wonderland* that he was primarily drawn but rather to tales of 'red Indians' and to the 'fairy books' of Scottish poet, novelist and literary critic Andrew Lang. These stories would form an indelible impression on his young mind which, coupled with the his exploration of the local countryside, would form the basis for some of his own literary works.

Tragedy struck the Tolkien household once again. When he was just twelve, Mabel, who as a single parent had inspired and supported him throughout his young life, died of acute diabetes at the age of just thirty-four. Prior to her death she had appointed a close friend, Father Francis Xavier Morgan of the Birmingham Oratory, to bring up her sons as good Catholics. As Tolkien would later write of the man he would call Father Francis:

"He was an upper-class Welsh-Spaniard Tory, and seemed to some just a pottering old gossip. He was - and he was not. I first learned charity and forgiveness from him; and in the light of it pierced even the 'liberal' darkness out of which I came, knowing more about 'Bloody Mary' than the Mother of Jesus - who was never mentioned except as an object of wicked worship by the Romanists."

Tolkien grew up in the Edgbaston area of Birmingham where he lived near Perrott's Folly and the Victorian tower of Edgbaston Waterworks. These two imposing structures may have influenced the images of the dark towers within his works. He also started to visit the Birmingham Museum and Art Gallery which had extensive collections of the romantic medievalist paintings of Edward Burne-Jones and the Pre-Raphaelite Brotherhood which, again, would forge strong impressions on his young mind and later in his own fantasy sagas.

Whilst still just a teenager, Tolkien first learned about constructed languages through the example of Animalic which had been created by his cousins, Mary and Marjorie Incledon. They would soon discard their creation, but Tolkien was fascinated by artificial languages and went on to invent his own much more complex creations, Nevbosh and Naffarin. He learned Esperanto, itself an artificially created language, in 1909 and shortly after wrote *The Book of Foxrook*, a sixteen page notebook containing a mixture of his own invented forms and Esperanto.

In 1911, whilst still attending St. Edward's School, where he formed a fellowship of literary minded friends that would be the forerunner Oxford's Inkling Society, a group that also include his good friend and fellow academic C.S. Lewis. He also developed an interest in poetry.

Tolkien found time to holiday in Switzerland where, he notes in a letter sent to his Hilary in 1968, that Bilbo's trek through the Misty Mountains in *The Hobbit* was directly inspired by his adventures with a party of twelve hikers on their way from Interlaken to Lauterbrunnen.

In October 1911, Tolkien was admitted to Exeter College, Oxford, where he studied Classics until he decided to change his course in 1913 to English and Language and Literature for which he graduated with a first in 1915.

Tolkien married Edith Mary Bratt, much to the displeasure of his guardian Father Francis, in a Catholic ceremony in 1913. Despite having no job, money or prospects, he settled happily into married life but just a year later the First World War was to change his outlook on life irrevocably and begin a journey that would end with the publication of *The Lord of The Rings* exactly forty years later. Yet, according to Tolkien, his terrifying experiences at the Somme did not directly inspire the creation of his greatest literary work. Indeed, he would later chastise those *The Lord of The Rings* fans who saw the novel as a missive against world war: in this case the Second World War which he also survived.

Indeed, it was during his times away from the Front and on trips home that he found inspiration for passages within LOTR. During his recovery from the effects of the First World War, in a cottage in Little Haywood, Staffordshire, he started work on 'The Book of Lost Tales', an attempt to create a mythology for England. He was never to finish it but some of the stories within it, such as 'The Fall of Gondolin', would be hinted at in later works.

Events during that period would also forge impressions that found their way into *The Lord of The Rings*. After being promoted to the temporary rank of Lieutenant in 1918, he was stationed at Kingston-upon-Hull. One day, during a walk with his wife through the woods at Roos, they stopped at a clearing where Edith began to dance for him amongst the Hemlock flowers. He remembers this day shortly after Edith's death in 1971 when he had the name of one of the great characters of Middle-earth carved upon her headstone:

"I never called Edith Luthien. It was first conceived in a small woodland glade filled with hemlocks[65] at Roos in Yorkshire (where I was for a brief time in command of an outpost of the Humber Garrison in 1917, and she was able to live with me for a while). In those days her hair was raven, her skin clear, her eyes brighter than you have seen them, and she could sing - and dance.".

This incident inspired the account of the meeting of Beren and Lúthien in *The Lord of The Rings* and Tolkien's history of the foundation of Middle-earth, *The Silmarillion*.

In November, 1920, Tolkien left the army and began work at The Oxford English Dictionary, looking at the etymology of words. Later that year he took up a post as Reader in English Language at the University of Leeds where he co-wrote the definitive edition of *Sir Gawain and the Green Knight*. He returned to Oxford in 1925, becoming Professor of Anglo Saxon at Pembroke College. During that time, and whilst resident at 20 Northmoor Road, North Oxford, he wrote *The Hobbit* and two thirds of *The Lord of The Rings*.

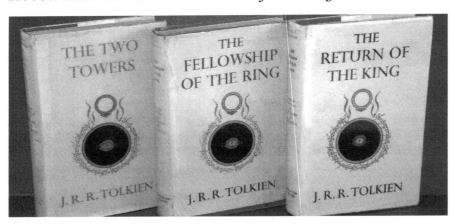

In 1945, after the Second World War, during which he acted as a cryptographer, he became Professor of English Language and Literature at Merton College, Oxford and completed *The Lord of The Rings* in 1948, nearly a decade after first putting rune to paper. The book was deemed too large by publisher Unwin & Allen so was eventually split into three volumes as a sequel to his children's book, *The Hobbit*, which had been published in 1937.

The Fellowship of The Ring was published on July 29th, 1954, *The Two Towers* on November 11th of that same year and *The Return of The King* almost a year later on October 20th, 1955. Tolkien had originally intended the novel to be published as one volume of a two-volume set, the other being *The Silmarillion*, but, again, his publisher was reluctant to proceed with such a large speculative project given that nothing similar had been published before. The final three volume set would later be joined by *The Silmarillion* and Tolkien continued to work on what he called the mythopoeia of Middle-earth right up to his death on September 2nd, 1973. Whilst he was then living in Bournemouth, his family decided to inter him at Wolvercote Cemetery in his beloved Oxford. Christopher, his son, then took on the mantle of his father's work, seeing *The Silmarillion* through to publication and keeping fans happy with a series of books covering the history, myths and legends of Middle-earth, the latest of which, *Beren and Lúthien,* was published in June 2017.

JRR Tolkien continues to be the father of the modern fantasy story, his books having sold nearly two hundred million copies worldwide and at the start of this month a new exhibition of the artwork and manuscripts he created during the writing and publication of *The Lord of The Rings* has opened at The Bodleian Library in Oxford. 'Tolkien: Maker of

Middle-earth' runs until October 28th, 2018 and can be booked online at https://tolkien.bodleian.ox.ac.uk/.

POLAND'S POET OF DARKNESS

Trevor Kennedy chats to Polish poet of the macabre,
Norbert Gora.

TK: It's a pleasure to speak with you, Norbert. You have contributed many excellent works to anthologies the world over, on top of your own solo books. What are you currently working on and when will it be released?

Norbert Gora: On 22nd March I announced that I wouldn't be writing horror any more. My statement appeared after a period of many unpleasant experiences in my life. I thought horror was over for me, but forward to two months later and I'm about to drop my first horror short story collection, *Brutality* (sadly, but it will only be available in Polish), and my first Polish poetry collection, *Praise of Darkness*. Looks like I can't live without horror.

TK: Have you always written and from what age did you find that you were a natural at verse?

Norbert Gora: I started writing as a teenager, but these were rather unsuccessful attempts. I wrote a few science fiction short stories. My friends liked those pieces, but from the perspective of time they were nothing more than crap. After a few long years I decided to go back to writing, including poetry. In 2015, when I was twenty-five, I realized that creating verses is something natural to me.

TK: What attracts you to the horror genre? Have you always been into darker subject matter?

Norbert Gora: No, not exactly. My first love in literature was science-fiction. I was so absorbed by the themes of time travelling, aliens, predictions of the future. I didn't even think about the power of horror. Everything changed though, when I read one of Dean Koontz's novels. Then it was over. The world of the darkness had already devoured me.

TK: You have had your work published across the globe in several different languages. Aside from your native Polish, which language do you find the easiest to write in?

Norbert Gora: I like writing poetry in English, but – in fact – it's a difficult language. Sometimes, when I write a poem, I send it to one of my editors, just to check the tense etc. The editor sends it back with questions like, 'What do you mean by your use of this word?'. It's kinda funny. Writing poetry in Polish – obviously – it's easier for me, but there are not many chances to do it, to publish it.

TK: Although you write mainly poetry, have you ever branched out into other literary fields, such as the penning of short stories or even a novel, for example?

Norbert Gora: Yes, of course. I've written a dozen short stories, but they appeared only in Polish. I have also a short story and a few flash fictions available in English, released mainly by Horrified Press. I would like to write a crime novel very soon.

TK: Poetry is a very specific writing form, something which I have never seriously attempted myself. What advice would you give any upcoming new poet?

Norbert Gora: You must feel it with your heart. Writing prose is based on action, on developing characters, describing places etc. You can always improve your skills, but poetry is composed of emotions. You must set them free, play with words, exaggerate trivialities and trivialize seriousness. It's a difficult, demanding art. If you're not ready, you shouldn't start.

 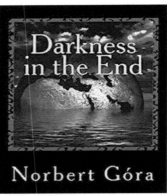

TK: Which form (or stanza perhaps) of verse do you prefer writing in?

Norbert Gora: I like both – rhymes and free verses.

TK: I studied Irish poetry a little at school and college and enjoy many of the popular classics, but if I am completely honest, poetry is not my area of expertise. Whose poetry do you enjoy reading for yourself?

Norbert Gora: Welcome in the club, ha! Well, Poland is the motherland of famous, worldwide known poets like Czesław Miłosz and Wisława Szymborska. I didn't like doing analysis of poetry, but it has changed a lot. Now we are heading for simplification in literature, for tearing metaphors and replacing them with words without imaginings. That's why I decided to write dark poetry. There is still a lot of place for the beauty of creativity with it. What is more, I think we can find here another slot – describing one of the worst diseases in the world – depression. It's important to speak about it, as loud as we can, but modern humanity is not interested.

I like reading poetry of Ashley Dioses, K.A. Opperman, Frank Coffman. All are involved in the horror genre.

TK: Norbert, it has been a joy chatting to you and we at Phantasmagoria Magazine wish you the greatest success in the future.

(Now turn the page to read some of Norbert's unpublished works).

*****

NOW ON SALE FROM AMAZON, THE NEW DARK COMEDY NOVEL FROM ADRIAN BALDWIN...

AVAILABLE IN PAPERBACK AND ON KINDLE

DARK POETRY CORNER

WITH NORBERT GORA

CONCUBINE OF NECROSIS

One-to-one trysts that were too weird
to understand how those feelings appeared,
the light of beauty met the darkness of eyesore,
innocence tasted the filthy bitterness of gore.

In the arms of death she quickly forgets
about the sort of things that can upset,
she worships the smell of decaying meat
when the slimy tongue touches her teat.

Longing washes her body during the day,
at night she loves the carcass, to whom she obeys,
infatuated and blissful, concubine of necrosis
submerges in the source of lifeless hypnosis.

With each grain of time her face becomes paler,
brighter than the fabric kept in the hands of tailor,
with every sunset, such a visible difference
between them disappears, fatal severance.

I'M NOT LIKE THEM

When night takes over
the vastness of the sky,
I put my fragile soul
on the other side.

It isn't more than a broken fabric,
wet from stored tears,
but their bitterness powers the mind
that can lift the mundane blockades.

I listen to the golden lips of this world
about separation of the body from the soul,
reason is tired of waiting
for the absolute of enlightenment.

Streets cluttered by nonsense
are a fuse to my anger,
I would like to bring death
to those void of awareness.

I'm not like them,
eulogists of doubt,
before the night rests, entombed by the day,
the knowledge previously unavailable
will be made known to me.

THE LAST NIGHT IN SPACE

Drifting ship full of agony
emerged from behind
a cloud of cosmic dust,
maybe hope died on board,
but the avalanche of sounds
still washes dirty steel.

The buzzer's cogs get into the mind
more than a long devil's claw,
the chopping generator spits out life,
with every grinding dread rising in us.

An electronic voice of indifference
whispers words swollen from memories,
dying so far from home, disturbed breathing
is louder than a volcanic explosion.

The last night in space, halfway to dreams,
accompanied by crying and crackling machines,
the howling siren disperses the red glow,
it is the arrow of death fired from a bow.

THE INVISIBLE PRINCE [1]

by David A. Sutton

As the red-tinted highlights of the setting sun caught the many windows of the city and the tumult of everyday life steadily settled, so a certain man put on his overcoat as he stood in his house in that fashionable part of the town. The fiery glory of the sunset gave way to grey dusk and the man, a recluse and haunter of the twilight, issued forth from his home and, veiled by night's early shadows, walked out into the street. In the less frequented parts of the city, over cobbled alleyways — the buildings absorbing the sombre tones of the encroaching night — the tall, handsome figure strode, casting a balefully thin shadow. Finally, he came upon one of his favourite haunts, a small, dilapidated bookshop. He entered the gloomy, musty-smelling interior of the establishment and asked the proprietor with a smile, *"Any more ghost stories for me?"* The bookseller immediately slipped into the darkness created by the ranks of leather-bound volumes and after a few minutes emerged into the diffused light again and gave the man several books. The tall customer would linger awhile, eagerly devouring the tales of supernatural terror and occult knowledge that the proprietor had handed to him...

The paragraph above could describe a town in New England, Providence, during the early 1930s and it could be a portrayal of the nocturnal habits of H. P. Lovecraft, that contemporary giant of the horror story. But in fact, the city is Dublin in the 1870s and the character is, of course, Joseph Sheridan Le Fanu.

This colourful vision may be overly dramatic, but in his last sixteen years, Le Fanu did withdraw from society, saw few people, was haunted by dreams, and evoked many of his ghostly tales as the result of these nightmares. This reclusiveness earned Le Fanu the romantic nickname of 'The Invisible Prince'. Of course, taken together, his business interests and financial problems, bringing up his four children (his wife had died in 1858) and the completion of ten novels and a string of short stories might have kept anyone away from the social round.

Sheridan Le Fanu came into the world on 28th August 1814, the son of Philip Le Fanu, then chaplain at the Royal Hibernian Military School in the Phoenix Park, Dublin. His ancestry could be traced to Caen in Normandy, as far back as the fifteenth century, the family being of Huguenot descent. In the seventeenth century, Charles Le Fanu de Cresserons, a Huguenot refugee, settled in Ireland and his grandson left a large amount of property to the family in Dublin and environs.

Even in his early years Le Fanu had a liking for solitude — although he had an elder sister and a younger brother — and when unwilling to see visitors he would retire to a room at the top of the house, which could only be reached by a retractable ladder. When Le Fanu was twelve years old, the family moved to Abington, six miles from Dublin and there his tutor idled his time, leaving the young gentleman and his brother to their own devices. However, this lack of schooling did nothing to affect Le Fanu's absorption of knowledge, for he would read without restriction in his father's large and well-stocked library, where he found books on demonology, the occult and folklore, which would later provide a foundation for his inclinations to write macabre stories and novels.

During his boyhood, Le Fanu was also to hear the mysterious oral tales and superstitions of the people, the folklore that was his country's rich heritage, with stories of ghosts and banshees and the ghostly riders, or 'phookas'. One of Le Fanu's biographers, S. M. Ellis wrote on this point:

"Only a few years were to elapse after his boyhood passed before he wrote down and embellished with supreme artistry these aural tales [the wild legends, superstitions and ghost stories of Ireland] he had loved in his childhood; and then, with increasing power of composition he went on to the creation of some of the greatest stories of mystery and the supernatural ever written in any language. As in the case of the most imaginative writers, Le Fanu owed a great deal to his irregular education and escape from the hide-bound moulds and individuality slaying codes of boarding schools." [2]

Le Fanu entered the university, Trinity College, Dublin, in the 1830s and there distinguished himself with his speeches for the college historical society. Although he began writing stories for publication soon after he graduated from Trinity College in 1837, he was at the time training to be a lawyer, but instead took up journalism. He bought a number of journals published in Dublin, notably the *Dublin Evening Mail*.

In 1844 he married Susan Bennett and they had four children, two sons and two daughters. (One of his sons, George Brinsley, became a well-known artist in the black and white medium and created several illustrations for his father's stories). This happy marriage was obliterated when, in 1858, Le Fanu's wife died and he retired to the seclusion of number eighteen Merrion Square, Dublin, where he stayed for the rest of his life.

It was in 1845 that he began publishing the first of his fourteen novels, but after the second, two years later, he left novel writing severely alone for fourteen years. Of his longer works, only three are considered to be his great achievement in that form, *The House by the Churchyard*, (1861) *Uncle Silas* (1864) and *Wylder's Hand* (1864). Le Fanu is more fondly remembered for his short stories of terror and the supernatural. The recent three-volume Ash-Tree Press editions, each with a detailed introduction to the author's life and works by Jim Rockhill, will readily attest to the significance of Le Fanu on supernatural literature.[3]

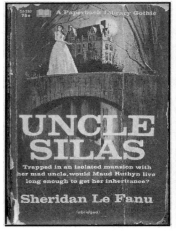 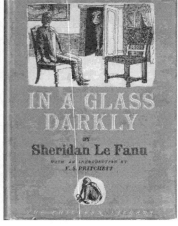

In 1861 Le Fanu became editor and proprietor of *The Dublin University Magazine* and it was in this auspicious publication that the bulk of his writing appears. He owned the magazine until about 1869 when he sold it, and from then onwards his tales were published in various other periodicals of his day.

During the last few years of his life, Le Fanu was so preoccupied with the supernatural that all the stories he wrote then confirmed this obsession. He became strongly influenced by the doctrines of the Swedish philosopher, Emmanuel Swedenborg. Swedenborg was an eighteenth century medium and clairvoyant, though by no means was he a Spiritualist Medium in the usual sense of the term, because Spiritualism did not emerge until the mid-nineteenth century. Through his dreams, visions and ecstatic trances, Swedenborg evolved a Christian doctrine about which Colin Wilson writes:

"The real importance of Swedenborg lies in the doctrines he taught, which are the reverse of the gloom and hell-fire of other breakaway sects. He rejects the notion that Jesus died on the cross to atone for the sin of Adam, declaring that God is neither vindictive nor petty-minded, and that since he is God, he doesn't need atonement. It is remarkable that this common-sense view had never struck earlier theologians. God is Divine Goodness, and Jesus is Divine Wisdom, and Goodness has to be approached through Wisdom. Whatever one thinks about the extraordinary claims of its founder, it must be acknowledged that there is something very beautiful and healthy about the Swedenborgian religion. This feeling of breezy health is the basic reason for its enduring popularity. Its founder may not have been a great occultist, but he was a great man." [4]

Le Fanu's interest in this strange mystic, his seclusion from the world and his interest in the weird and the occult in general must all have deeply wrought themselves on his imagination and the result are some of the best ghost stories ever written. Even his method of writing must have allowed those cold shadows of horror to impinge upon his consciousness and, referring again to his biographer S. M. Ellis, here is a description of Le Fanu's method:

"He wrote mostly in bed at night, using copy-books for his manuscript. He always had two candles by his side on a small table; one of these dimly glimmering tapers would be left burning while he took a brief sleep. Then, when he awoke about two a.m. amid the darkling shadows of the heavy furnishings and hangings of his old-fashioned room, he would brew himself some strong tea which he drank copiously and frequently throughout the day and write for a couple of hours in that eerie period of the night when human vitality is at its lowest ebb and the Powers of Darkness rampant and terrifying."

Ellis reported that at the end of his life Le Fanu suffered from the plague of a recurring dream, in which a crumbling old mansion was about to fall and crush him. This horrible nightmare was communicated to his doctor, who said, when Le Fanu died on 9th February 1873, "I feared this – that house fell at last". Alas, this anecdote cannot be substantiated from any other source, so we have to accept that perhaps S. M. Ellis embellished his biography. Needless to say, the author's stories stand above any such romantic embroideries and whatever other atmospheric assertions are made about Le Fanu's life.

Le Fanu was at the peak of his creative skill during the period 1861-1872, where his narrative flair and the ingenuity of his terrors are at their most malevolent. 'The Child That Went with The Fairies' (1870) for instance, is a dreamy, haunting story featuring one of the most potent myths that Le Fanu would have heard in his youth from his elders. Despite our latter-day exposure to fairies as pleasant delicate creatures of the Cottingley variety, this tale harks back to the real nature of the 'little folk', (the sort that Arthur Machen told of so well) and the bizarre group of fairies who steal away a child in this story are far from pleasant.

Even in one of his earliest published stories, 'Schalken the Painter' (1851) the author demonstrates those elements which occur in much of his later work: the grotesque perambulations of the dead and their ability to manipulate psychic forces; the evil contract entered into (whether on paper or aurally agreed upon) by the unsuspecting protagonist; and the subtle, erotic undertones which Le Fanu blends with his deftly etched horrors. Schalken, whose morbid paintings set the story in motion, is a subsidiary character until the revelation at the story's end, when his lost love, Rose Velderkaust reveals the awful secret of her grim spouse. In his biography, Nelson Browne commented on the story, "This strange tale, with its hint of demoniacal possession and its charnel house atmosphere, is Le Fanu's first essay in his most horrible vein, and although there is little evidence of the finesse that he achieved in later examples the impressiveness is lasting."

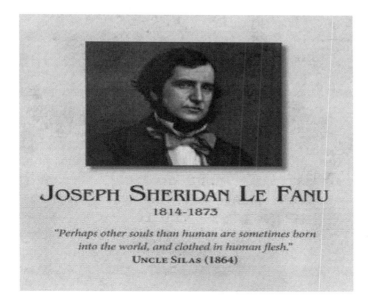

JOSEPH SHERIDAN LE FANU
1814-1873

"Perhaps other souls than human are sometimes born into the world, and clothed in human flesh."
UNCLE SILAS (1864)

Le Fanu has found lasting fame through his shorter works, though it was not always so. Nelson Browne, in his biography, had this to say about the author:

"Even in his own lifetime Le Fanu was not a popular author.

His skill in creating ghosts and exploiting the horrible and macabre is of such a delicate and unobtrusive kind that it has always failed to attract the notice of those, whose tastes, if they tend in this direction at all, have no palate for subtle flavours." And further: "Le Fanu, with fourteen novels and at least two-score shorter pieces, was the equal of the most prolific of the great Victorian writers in output alone, but the Victorian reading public preferred something more robust, less pessimistic, less psychologically disturbing. On the other hand, we today, less psychologically stable and at the same time more worldly-wise than the Victorians when it comes to dealing with neuroses, are more attuned to Le Fanu's quiet yet restless undertones." [5]

It is certainly true that, although written over one hundred and fifty years ago, many of these stories hold a timeless quality whose subtle and demoniac characters, despite the affectations of the literature of the day, find ready entry into our contemporary and disordered cosmos. 'Ultor de Lacy' (1861) is the nightmarish account of an ancient and noble Irish family who, having come upon hard times, dwell in a part of the sequestered, twilit rooms of their ancestral home, while round about, the intrusion of a malignant and spectral figure weaves a web of doom. De Lacy is bequeathed a legacy from his dying father, that terrified him in some way when he heard of it as a boy, and only later in the story do we see the result of this fearful bequest. What the former de Lacy did to bring upon his son and his two beautiful daughters the wrath of this demon is hinted at, but around this is the aura of the ghostly ruin of the ancient castle and the rocky glen from which it protrudes, a place of sunset shadows and unhealthy phenomena; a place which itself can disappear from mortal sight.

However, despite the lasting reputation Le Fanu has achieved, even in 1974 it was considered that devotees of the ghost and horror story undervalued his work. In my own fantasy literature review, *Shadow* (1968-74), the very last issue contained an appreciation of the author written by one of his own countrymen, Patrick Quigley, in which he said in part:

"He was a strange and eccentric man; intelligent; possessing a sense of humour and of honesty; inclined to morbidness and mildly paranoid; conservative, yet he wasn't afraid to introduce sexual elements into his writings. As with the best of horror writers he takes great care with descriptive detail, so that an amazingly clear picture of the background to the stories emerges to be absorbed by our minds in which curiosity has been aroused. As we go through this world of the past there is not the dusty heaviness that confronts us in history books... It's surprising that he could be so neglected even by weird fantasy readers. There are many similarities between Le Fanu and Lovecraft – their interest in ancient architecture and antiquity, and in their habit of application to detail and portentous hints in their writings. Furthermore, they both evolved a definite standpoint in regard to the supernatural that was naturally their own. While Lovecraft opted for the view of man in a dark, chaotic universe, Le Fanu took a more ordered view of things." [6]

The title 'Green Tea' (1869) refers to a beverage taken in excessive quantities by the unfortunate clergyman in the story, who is haunted by a particularly malevolent demon. Its form would be common enough were other circumstances prevailing than those of a supernatural manifestation. Le Fanu also used this theme in another of his tales, 'The Watcher', (also revised and published as 'The Familiar') and both are regarded among his most popular stories. 'Green Tea' is the more intriguing, yet both display a prosaic approach to the preternatural compared to some of his less well-remembered stories. The prologue to this and certain other of Le Fanu's tales features a certain Dr. Hesselius, a German physician skilled in psychiatry and the occult sciences. According to Nelson Browne, this character represents the author himself, with a dash of Swedenborgian speculation thrown in for good measure.

For some time, the bulk of Le Fanu's shorter work was not

known to be his, much of it being published anonymously in the journals of his day. Le Fanu had kept accurate records of all his literary transactions, but these were lost after his death. Important work was laboriously undertaken by M. R. James, who unearthed and published some notable stories in the collection *Madam Crowl's Ghost & Other Tales of Mystery* [7]. In this collection M. R. James says of its author, "He stands absolutely alone in the first rank as a writer of ghost stories... Nobody sets the scene better than he, nobody touches in the effective detail more deftly." Praise, indeed, from one whose own work in the realm of the ghostly tale is considered to be rarely surpassed. The title story, 'Madame Crowl's Ghost' is a most fascinating one, in which is displayed a compulsion for the grotesque, couched in Le Fanu's beautifully underplayed style. The story is remarkable in that the ghost, as it were a second-hand one, is merely the catalyst in which the author intertwines a tale of malevolence, insanity, murder and gruesome discoveries.

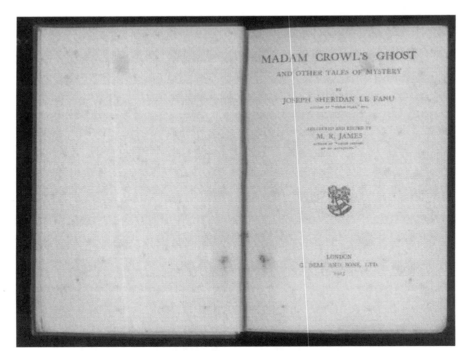

'The Dead Sexton' (1871) is one of Le Fanu's stories about the village of Golden Friars, here coated in the crisp winter monochrome of moonlight and snow. It has its friendly, homely George and Dragon Inn, the cosy turf fire and the smell of hot punch on the kitchen air. The sexton of the village, a morose individual, robbed of his life by a grisly accident while he was himself robbing the church of its bells, lies in the inn stable to await the coroner, when into the village sweeps a mysterious rider mounted on a huge black stallion. What his business is in Golden Friars is revealed by the chill atmosphere of winter's night as the innkeeper waits up to keep an eye on the sexton's corpse.

'Sir Dominick's Bargain' (1872), a story about a pact with Satan in return for wealth, is told not by the comfort of a roaring fire; the unfortunate recipient instead hears the fate of Sir Dominick at the very scene of his gruesome end. Dunoran House, in ruins, sets a baleful, forbidding scene, a lonely pile, wherein the grim double-cross played by Satan finds fruition.

'Carmilla' (1871-72) is Le Fanu's masterwork of his shorter pieces. Not only this, but one of the most profound and important vampire stories ever written. It predates Bram Stoker's *Dracula* by some twenty-six years and the author's research into vampire lore is abundantly exploited. 'Carmilla', by stages, by degrees exquisite in its hair-tingling excitement, reveals the illicit, shocking and lesbian eroticism of the beautiful vampire. The author, with astonishing subtlety creates a moving, nightmarish and sexually charged story that invokes its hypnotic spell as easily as Carmilla raids the virtues of her helpless and entranced victims. At one time Le Fanu reveals his monster to be just that — disposing of her victims with tasteless brevity. Then, in demoniacally capricious mood, to savour the pleasurable, sensuous delight of making her favourite victim join with her in a joyous, endless passion wherein Carmilla's lust for blood is kept bubbling as an almost irrepressible undercurrent. Remembering that the story is some one hundred and fifty years old, it is a remarkably modern tale and its subtle blend of eroticism and horror assures it a ready place in our contemporary minds. Nelson Browne says that, "'Carmilla' is the quintessence of vampire lore. Less prolix than the time-honoured *Dracula*, less extravagant than the most thoroughgoing of all shockers, *Varney the Vampire*, it is at once distinguished from the crude 'feast of blood' variety of vampire stories by the plausibility of the narrative and by those touches of *funeste* horror which Le Fanu alone can produce."

DRAWN BY D. H. FRISTON. "CARMILLA." ENGRAVED BY G. M. JENKIN.

To appreciate Le Fanu's short supernatural fiction oeuvre, Ash-Tree Press' magnificent three-volume set is the best way to acquaint or reacquaint yourself with his work (see footnotes below). However, on a more modest budget second-hand copies of various titles can easily be obtained: *Best Ghost Stories of J. S. Le Fanu* and *Ghost Stories and Mysteries* are both edited by E. F. Bleiler, from Dover Books. *Madam Crowl's Ghost and Other Stories* and *In a Glass Darkly* are published by Wordsworth Classics. And from The Echo Library there's *J. S. Le Fanu's Ghostly Tales*. Sarob Press has also recently published *Carmilla* (1998) and *Spalatro: Two*

Italian Tales (2001) as two slim hardcover volumes.

So, 'The Invisible Prince', stalking through those shrouded Dublin streets, saw strange phantasms; observed supernatural splendour implicit in the wild and lonely hills; found friendly discourse with rampant ghouls and wicked but beautiful vampires; let himself be drawn away by fairy-folk in their resplendent coaches; in hidden glens he spied ancient castles whose walls concealed wraiths as substantial as the living occupants... As Patrick Quigley noted, "These stories venture dangerously close to the edge of madness because Le Fanu could mix reality and the unknown in a fashion that has been rarely equalled." And I think that's as succinct enough of an observation to end on.

Footnotes

1. I first commenced writing this article in the mid 1970s. At the time Corgi Books had embarked on a 'Masters of

Terror' series, of which the first volume, *William Hope Hodgson* (ed. Peter Tremayne), had been published in 1977. Although I was commissioned to select the stories for volume 2 and write the introduction, the publisher failed to follow through with any further volumes in the series. The nine stories I had selected for the collection were, 'Schalken the Painter', 'An Account of some Strange Disturbances in Aungier Street', 'Ultor de Lacy', 'Green Tea', 'The Child That Went With the Fairies', 'Madam Crowl's Ghost', 'The Dead Sexton', 'Sir Dominick's Bargain' and 'Carmilla'.

2. *Wilkie Collins, Le Fanu & Others*, by S. M. Ellis (Constable & Co, 1931).

3. *Schalken the Painter and Others: Ghost Stories 1838-61* (Ash-Tree Press 2002), *The Haunted Baronet and Others: Ghost Stories 1861-70* (Ash-Tree Press 2003), *Mr Justice Harbottle and Others: Ghost Stories 1870-73* (Ash-Tree Press 2005). Edited, with an extensive introduction in each volume by Jim Rockhill.

4. *The Occult* by Colin Wilson (Hodder and Stoughton 1971)

5. *Sheridan Le Fanu*, by Nelson Browne (Arthur Barker 1951)

6. *Le Fanu, An Appreciation* by Patrick Quigley (*Shadow Fantasy Literature Review* issue no. 21, August 1974).

7. *Madam Crowl's Ghost & Other Tales of Mystery*, edited by M. R. James (G. Bell & Sons Ltd, 1923).

(**David A. Sutton** lives in Birmingham, England. He is the recipient of the World Fantasy Award, The International Horror Guild Award and twelve British Fantasy Awards for editing magazines and anthologies (*Fantasy Tales, Dark Voices: The Pan Book of Horror* and *Dark Terrors: The Gollancz Book of Horror*). Other anthologies include *New Writings in Horror & the Supernatural, The Satyr's Head & Other Tales of Terror, Phantoms of Venice* and *Haunts of Horror*. He has also been a genre fiction writer since the 1960s with stories appearing widely in anthologies and magazines, including in *Best New Horror, Final Shadows, The Mammoth Book of Merlin, Beneath the Ground, Shadows Over Innsmouth, The Black Book of Horror, Subtle Edens, The Ghosts & Scholars Book of Shadows, Psychomania, Second City Scares* and *Kitchen Sink Gothic*. His short stories are collected in *Clinically Dead & Other Tales of the Supernatural* and *Dead Water and Other Weird Tales*. He is also the proprietor of Shadow Publishing, a small press specialising in collections and anthologies).

*****

AVAILABLE SOON FROM AMAZON AND PRESENTED BY ZOMBIEPALOOZA RADIO PUBLISHING...

*****

PHANTASMAGORIA FICTION

First up, an exclusive extract from the brand new international anthology, **GRUESOME GROTESQUES VOLUME 3: CODEX GIGAS (TALES OF THE OCCULT)**, now on sale from Amazon and Forbidden Planet, Belfast in paperback and on Kindle.

ALPHABET OF DESIRE

by John Gilbert

"What is the weight of a soul, the substance of a spirit? And can you measure it?" I lean back in my seat and study Alesha's face for the arrival of an answer. The girl has been so good in her exposition of Buddhist philosophy and expertly subtle in the communication of her sexual identity, but loses it where supernature and quantum physics intersect.

"I don't think you can quantify it if you're talking about something supernatural beyond the natural world. Maybe we can't measure it."

Okay, so I am wrong. Alesha can extend logic beyond textbook answers. I smile, admitting the possibility of a good answer. I cough and the slight breeze from the ferry's air conditioning rubs razor chills against my neck turning my whole body to shivers that I quickly cover with a reply. "But, the soul could be so light that it's immeasurable by mechanical or electrical devices."

Alesha shakes her head. "If scientists have found a way to look out at galaxies using theoretical equations then the same should be possible with the soul."

"What if it doesn't want to be found?" I ask. "If, when it's freed from the body it buys into the whole afterlife and suddenly knows why it must move on or stay hidden."

It was all bullshit of course, well, most of it, but bullshit that was going to keep Alesha at my side until we docked at the Hook of Holland. Bullshit of which even Weaver would have been proud, enough to mask my real purpose.

***

I hardly consider myself a pupil though on occasion Weaver had fondly called me 'Chela', a novice in the mystic arts. My reticence in accepting the accolade was not through any lack of self esteem, but rather because of the place in which the knowledge was imparted. Prison was a learning experience in itself and degraded the process if not the content.

Still, Weaver was keen to pass on his knowledge and I to accept it because it kept my mind from my sick body's incarcerated state. More importantly, it freed me from the dangerous vacuum of individual thought that can occur, like an epileptic fit, at any time on the inside. At first I thought Weaver's lessons were for my benefit but then I realised he was only preparing me for his own purpose.

He had initially taken pity on me, after lock-up sitting on the lower bunk and massaging away the bruises I had received from another of Annil's morning beatings. "You don't have to be this weak, you know: There are ways of surviving that the little thug wouldn't understand."

The desperation in my face must have trumpeted my readiness to accept anything but another beating. His gangly arms tensed, veins slipping against unnourished muscle, when he pushed himself off the bunk and snatched up the battered pad of paper and pencil from the cell's one table.

He dented the paper with thick strokes, creating a simple but unintelligible mandala of circles, squares and triangles. Finally, a single flourish produced a tilting swirl that could have been a signature, but certainly not his own.

Weaver sighed and straightened up, the growing intensity in his arms, hands and eyes suddenly vanishing. He passed the picture to me and smiled.

I looked down at this doodle, unsure how to react and

flinched a moment later when I realised he was talking to me.

"At the turn of the twentieth century they used to think that real magic was achieved with robes, ceremonial and occult grades of greatness. Huge organisations like The Golden Dawn and OTO drew rich patrons who funded temples and lodges.

Everything, beautifully ornate. Problem was that these groups only proclaimed the richer patrons as adepts: the magic was weak and unfocused.

Then the likes of Aleister Crowley broke away and formed their own theologies of magic - Crowley even added a 'k' to his brand to distinguish it from the others. He worked with the mind and symbols rather than outside props, bit like the virtual reality researchers do now for computer companies.

He wasn't alone. Many from the London artists' colonies founded their own magical systems, including a man called Austin Osman Spare. He had discovered that using symbols keyed in to the human subconscious you could do all sorts of magic. He was able to summon the strength of a tiger, the calm or cunning of a snake, the wisdom of an elephant. He believed it was all there in our past waiting to be summoned; called it Atavistic Resurgence. He and others like him created alphabets that they could use to fashion their desires, their fantasies, into reality. It's even believed that he might have used one of his symbols to move his life force into another body when he was dying. What amazing magick that would be."

I mouthed the words, their meaning still far from me.

"He even conjured a rose out of thin air."

I couldn't help laughing, "A rose. Why not something more useful."

My blunt disbelief did not appear to anger or put him off. He tapped at the paper. "The symbol's like a visual spell. All you have to do is internalise it so that you can imagine it when you close your eyes."

"And what then?"

"When you can replicate it well enough in your mind and have given it time to key into your subconscious, all you need to do is concentrate on the symbol and you summon the strength, the magic, within you."

"Oh yeah?" The smirk on my face must have hinted that I was unconvinced. His habit of mixing tall tales with truth - a habit shared with the infamous Aleister Crowley, he had once told me - left me nervous about believing everything said. Yet, that confident smile of his, visible only when he knew he had won, never flickered as he left me alone in the cell.

***

Alesha, has pleasure mapped into her flesh, the sureness of a whore, tempered with whispers of innocence. She is the lover I craved in prison before I settled for Weaver's friendship, and now I want to take just a little longer in her company.

I still adore my prison-side mentor, will do anything for him, but such young company - mind, spirit as well as skin - is rare in my experience. I need to savour it for just a while. After all, Weaver has strived ten years for freedom: He can wait a little longer – at least until we get to Amsterdam.

***

I did not choose the violence. The opportunity was there and it chose me.

For three weeks I learned the symbol that Weaver had drawn, concentrating on its rough spiky uniqueness with a determination I had lost at my sentencing.

Prison became a portal, my cell a cabin from which I rarely ventured. The screws frowned every time they poked their heads around the door to announce lock-up and my personal officer eventually gave up asking if I was hiding from someone.

Oh yes, I was hiding, but not from any nightmare that place could conjure. Weaver had told me to concentrate and also warned me not to let anyone else see the symbol: such discovery would diffuse its power. So I hid it in my shoe where sweat made it damp and, eventually smudged each of its thick pencilled contours.

The sharp, defined image remained fresh in my mind and, when the time came to use it, I was surprised at the speed with which I could conjure its presence.

It was coincidence rather than force of will that finally brought this power into use.

Eric Flynn was a quiet loner yet he had a voice, his fists, and they gave him the say of any animal prison gang. It must have been my upcoming release date that awoke him to my presence within the prison system. In the past he had simply pushed me aside if I had gotten in his way. Relieved as I was that he was not interested in me, I had never worried about these assaults, but when he started to see the possibilities in my release I began to dread his presence.

Flynn needed a link to the outside and, having no natural friends, saw the opportunity to mark me as an unnatural ally. Several times he threatened me at meal breaks and then, two weeks before I got out, he came to my cell when Weaver was away.

The first I knew of his presence was the dull clang of the door closing. Then the smell of his aftershave - stolen, no doubt from Boris on C Wing who always reeked of the stuff - preceded his thick fingers wringing the flesh of my arm. I cried out, forced off balance to turn and face him.

"Hello," he whispered, in a voice that sounded as if it came from the bottom of a particularly rank well. "I think it's time we bonded."

I fell back against the hard-wire frame of the bottom bunk bed, certain of what he meant.

Not a word passed my lips as he approached, raising his arms to pull me out of my hole.

I flinched and retreated into the saving space between the bunks only to feel the twisting of my tee shirt in his fists as they pummelled my scrawny chest.

At that moment fear cancelled physical response and instinct took over. The image I had so carefully cultivated in the hope that it would mean something cascaded before my eyes.

I had expected to feel a sudden rush of brutal force through my body, readying it for combat, but instead my arms and legs relaxed, catching my assailant off centre.

He fell forward, lashed by my arms with such power that I almost did not hear the brittle crack of his jaw. He opened his mouth with a wail. Blood seeped between his teeth and peppered his chin as he staggered back.

My foot followed, toes twisting within sandals, bevelling viciously up and into the soft fat of his chest. He went down in a fit of coughing, drizzling dark liquid on the slick green floor.

The symbol, just one character from an alphabet of my desires, throbbed before me, its power inside. I rose, involuntarily clenching my fists, standing over my victim, prepared for him to fight back; but he did not.

My feeling of invincibility receded. I stepped back against the wall, wheezing and coughing.

All strength gone, feeble reality returned. Gasping for breath, I watched the only sign of movement from Flynn's body: the twitching fingers of his left hand pressed down against the floor and he pushed himself into a kneeling position. Bloody-faced, he looked up at me. Beaten for the first time in his five years in the system he did not know what to do. I pointed to the wash basin. "I'll be back later. You won't be here."

When I passed through the door and out onto the walkway I smiled, prayed, and worshipped Weaver.

***

I shake the spunk-filled condom into the sanitary bin by the sink and steady my quaking hands. The girl in the next room feebly calls my name. I ignore her, confident of the drugged vodka's power, that she will lose consciousness within the next two minutes.

If you are going to commit murder the one big problem is the body. That is one of Weaver's maxims. I believe him not because of any legal proof, any time done, or any rumours of bodies hidden, but because he is the sort of man who never asks someone else to do something unless he has been there himself.

Anyway, according to him this is not murder. And disposal of the body? I have no such concerns.

***

It was nearly teatime when I pushed open the metal door to my cell, half expecting to discover Flynn still bloodied-up but waiting for me. Instead I found the floor clear except for a dark red rose in full bloom where my nemesis had fallen.

I stooped and picked it up, wary that someone could be waiting for me to bare my back to violence. No such attack came so I slipped my fingers around the stem, resting the thick thorns carefully in the palm of my hand.

I realised someone had entered the cell, behind me. Instinctively I turned, the thorns slicing against my skin. I winced in pain then sighed with relief when I caught sight of Weaver's passive face. He was carrying a thick water-bloated paperback, Anne Rice's *The Body Thief*, his finger stuck as a marker in the middle.

"You?" I asked, raising the rose to eye level.

"Miraculous," he smiled.

"You've never given me a present before."

He blew an exaggerated kiss at me and held out the book. "A present and a promise of rewards to come".

***

I unzip the bulging leather carryall and pull the gunmetal case from beneath its covering of tee-shirts and jeans. As contraband it is not hidden too well but I have taken a risk that I would not be searched coming into the Hook of Holland.

Pulling the case open I stroke the two large syringes, both full of murky liquid. The first will relax the already sleeping girl even more; the second stop her lungs and heart. She will be dead in fifteen minutes, dead long enough for Weaver to take possession.

Efficient and, most importantly, one of the few ways to leave the central organs undamaged.

I cup the two syringes in my hand, walk back into the bedroom and, with just a glance at the beautiful naked body outstretched and peacefully unaware, I pick up the battered paperback from the bedside table.

"You're out in two weeks, I can be too - with your help." If Weaver had not prepared me I would not have believed.

"How?" I asked, knowing he had at least another seven years to serve before any hope of parole.

He sat beside me on the bunk and flicked through the book he had been carrying for the past week. His silence was unnerving.

"This involves me smuggling you out in some way?"

Weaver nodded and smiled. "But not at any risk of getting caught, I promise." He flapped the book and its thick pages rustled eerily against each other as he handed it to me. "Let it open in the middle."

I did as he asked, unsure of what I was expected to discover. The pages fell open where he had broken the spine and I was not altogether surprised to find one of his ornately drawn symbols on the right hand page.

"I haven't told you the half of what you can do with a symbol from our alphabet of desire. Yes, you can use them to cast what you call spells but you can also use them as doorways."

"Doorways?" I frowned.

"Yes, some call it the astral plane, others Akasha, psychology calls it the Great Unconscious, a space shared by all human beings. It's where we go when we dream, lands created by our own desires," He looked down at the book, "The only problem is that as with any dream you will spring back into the body, into waking consciousness - unless you die, and if you die you're normally stuck there."

I traced a fingertip along the edges and loops of the symbol -

the doorway - which seemed to act as a maze, sucking it in to the very heart of the design. "And how does that help you walk out of prison?"

"It doesn't. I don't walk. You're going to kill me."

***

I hold the first syringe up to the window light and rest my thumb on the plunger, conjuring the killing spirit with which I'd first become acquainted two months ago. Then I had been in the cell while Weaver's body - sans consciousness, spirit or soul - lay on the lower bunk. Death awaiting investigation by the authorities.

I look down at the battered paperback, the page at its centre containing the symbol, his portal between existences. And just on the other side, waiting to step into the girl, is his soul.

***

Kill me, he had said dispassionately and at that point I had felt like laughing: but I had believed enough to do it.

There had been no struggle, just a slight flopping movement of his bare arms when I pressed the pillow gently over his face. No evidence of violence, just lungs that had stopped breathing. No doubt there might have been the tell tale of exploded blood vessels somewhere, showing that the thin trail of life that remained had been extinguished by an outside agency. But, as Weaver had promised, all the authorities did was detain me for a few more weeks while a perfunctory investigation came to an inconclusive end.

***

I pick up the novel and look down at the symbol which Weaver had used as a doorway and spirit home at his death; this is his literary existence until he could project into the girl.

60

The symbol was one of several that Weaver had instructed me to teach this victim, this girl, seduced by the power of other symbols, other spells, amongst which a deadly trap door had been primed within her mind, a trapdoor through which he could spring into her mind, take possession of her body in the moments that her own spirit was extinguished.

Trashy: The kind of thing you read and discard. He had been so firm and assuring while we were together inside, always pointing out ways to survive. Yet, to be honest, I see he was only interested in his freedom, self-preservation.

We all are, aren't we?

I lift the page containing his symbol, the page impregnated with his discarnate soul, slip the lighter from my pocket and watch it burn. An imaginary male scream flickers in my mind: an apt fanfare to mark Weaver's passing.

Time to go.

I stroke the girl's helpless body: a film of warm sweat comes away on my greying fingertips.

A cough chatters through my lungs.

"Sorry," I whisper, and I am. At first I had thought twice about transferring to a female body. This girl was not as physically strong as a male body, but it had been the easiest to seduce, to ensnare in my current state. And, yes, I had thought twice about the ethics of it all. Truth and ethics had never bothered Weaver, or so he had told me. He had not believed in Karma; if it did exist, he had boasted he could divert even that natural law.

Yet, I am not a monster; just someone who wants to survive. When it comes to AIDS there is no greater need, no greater promise.

If science can't find an answer you create your own. Never mind that someone else, just as desperate, gives you the solution or that another - more innocent - must cease to exist to continue that chain of life. My life.

Despite the illness, I am more powerful than Weaver, more determined, and can easily smother the weak soul lying on the bed, eject it with a simple flick of my incorporeal mind.

The needles slip into my arm. There is no feeling of finality until that second plunger has been forced down. Then I lie back on the bed. My lungs feel heavy but not with the dread of asthma or pneumonia. No, here is a stifling relief that welcomes the brief transition of death, the promise for the soon to be reborn...

(**John Gilbert** has retired from editing to concentrate on his first love, writing. He is the creator and editor of *FEAR Magazine* and currently the consultant editor of *Phantasmagoria Magazine*. Based in Brighton, UK).

WIGGLE ROOM

by Christina Engela

Imagine, if you will:

In a true horror story there is no justice. There can't be, because a story where the evil villain gets their due in the end is too satisfying to the normal functioning mind. All the loose ends have been tied off, and all the reasons for the reader to be afraid have been neatly solved, packed away, archived, defused and eliminated.

No – in a horror, a *real* story, the villain gets away after having done some terrible thing, leaving the reader thrilled and horrified and the villain facing no consequences – being still at large and out there, lurking in the shadows of the mind. This offends the standard sensibility and leaves a story open ended, and not in a good way... Like a severed artery bleeding out, this is the real horror of it. This, dear reader, is one of those stories.

***

Cold. Wet. It was a clichéd dark and stormy night in a big city. A few street lights reflected in the water pooled in the streets, motionless except for the lashing rain and the wind wailing outside like a cold, hungry, homeless banshee, tearing at the hearts of children hiding in their beds. Our story begins here. It begins with a nurse.

Nosocomephobia – this is a little known word which is said to mean 'a fear of hospitals'. Whether or not this fear is a rational or irrational one... well, dear reader – that will be for you to decide... but before you do, let's take a closer look at the setting of our delightfully dark and deliciously demented tale:

The hospital was old, having a history most people didn't know – and even those who thought they did, didn't know the whole story. It was an old, old story – nearly as old as the city herself – and the back cover of the book was still splayed open, leaving this dark story exposed at its last page, unfinished – and leaving a sinister doorway ajar for it to leak out and taint the world with its venom.

The nurse walked down the corridors of the hospital, the rhythmic click of her high heels echoing eerily on the tiles and into the silent desolation of the wee hours of the night. Pale florescent lights made her pristine white uniform shine bright white – so white as to be almost obscene, like virgin snow, or something out of a clichéd commercial for fabric whitener. Black curls, medium length, were tightly styled down with hairspray and restrained by sharp hair pins. Her hands would have been white around the knuckles as they tightly gripped the bedpan, were they not already so deathly pale all over. She had dainty hands, and long fingers, the Nurse. They seemed manicured in their appearance, smooth in their youthfulness, and spotless – except where a little blood had gotten under her carefully shaped finger nails. The contented smile set across her lips – her crisply outlined, full, painted lips – indicated that she didn't mind. In fact, she enjoyed it.

The further she walked, rhythmically, steadily, inexorably, the more the fixtures and fittings along her route, both electrical and medical – and the architecture – began to resemble a Gothic, steampunk nightmare. Spider webs clung to the walls, hung from the ceilings, and decorated the ancient wooden door frames, brass light switches and outdated light fittings. Dust coated the floors, long un-swept, except for the motion of her passing. Here, in the older, abandoned part of this sprawling building, underground – where nobody was supposed to go anymore – where the lights were supposed to be off, creepy shadows danced and played on the walls. Strange whispers echoed faintly on the edge of hearing and faint movements that defied rational explanation danced just out of clear vision. The living no longer had any business here.

The old mortuary was a storeroom now – and had been for some decades, since the new section of the building had been built on. Even the administrators had forgotten what had been stored here, and had in turn with the passage of time, themselves been forgotten. The faded and peeling walls were long obscured by stacks and mountains of stored furniture: desks, chairs, rows of antique filing cabinets, and piles of boxes of discarded files and old archaic equipment, with the odd worn-out, dust-gray theater gown draped or hung over them. Long disused, the bank of ancient refrigerators stood empty – their battered old doors hanging forlornly open, telling the story of a journey traveled by so very many – who had apparently left the doors open behind them as though extending a chilling invitation to the world on the other side. That other world didn't seem that far away in places like this. It was like it could be on the other side of the door, that wall – or even in this room.

A giant spider seemed to be standing in the center of the room, an ancient theater light sort of thing with huge reflectors – some broken, but mostly still working. The light radiating from the reflectors spot-lit the dust bunnies and cobwebs that snaked across the rust and dust-covered steel. The Nurse walked towards it, almost gliding across the dusty floor, barely affecting the surface, carrying the bedpan – a look of anticipation on her crisp, perfect features.

James Booth's eyes flickered open. The lights were blinding. They were hot too, not like modern lights at all. They were blazing, almost singing him through the gaps in the broken lens covers. He struggled through the confusion. He remembered the car accident. It was night time, he was driving home alone – he remembered the dog running into the road ahead of him, swerving, the screeching of brakes, a tree on the side of the road – the awful jarring impact! He couldn't remember anything after that. Till now.

He couldn't move. Well, he could a little. He could – well, he could wiggle some. As much as his bonds would allow. Each arm was tied down beside him to something out of sight that didn't want to budge. The ropes around his wrists were tight. At least he thought they were ropes. For all he knew, they could have been nylon seat belts... Or duct tape.

His upper body felt naked, the skin on his back felt stuck to – what was that – vinyl? Old, cracked leather? His feet were tied down too, and the bed he was on – if it was a bed at all, squeaked and rattled and rocked considerably as he struggled. He couldn't see much, despite the blinding light that surrounded him. That would be due to the blindfold – a rough piece of material that appeared to have been wound around his head to cover his eyes, and knotted. There was a gap, positioned just so that he could see a tiny amount through it with one eye. A body board and restraints were pretty much to be expected for such a collision, he knew. He'd watched enough medical emergency TV series to know that. But he had no neck brace – and he was pretty sure the blindfold wasn't standard issue! He cried out – in confusion, but mostly in terror – but some kind of hard thing that tasted like plastic or rubber had been forced into his mouth, stifling him. Definitely not standard issue!

His heart was racing, his breathing labored – and under the blindfold, his eyes were opened wide, searching. His ears, straining, heard his own breathing. What was that? *Whimpering? Pathetic!* He heard his inner macho cursing. *Fucking pathetic!*

Then he heard it. Faint. In the distance, growing gradually louder. Rhythmic. The sound of shoes clicking in the distance. High heeled women's shoes!

"Hello?" He called in his head, even as his ears heard his own pathetic muffled cries. "Help!"

The clicking of the heels grew closer and closer, keeping the same detached and intimidating rhythm throughout his vain struggling, punctuated with the clanks and squeaks of the bed or bench he was strapped to. He broke into a sweat. Closer and closer they came, until they stopped somewhere near his feet. He ceased the pointless struggling to try to see the body attached to the shoes he'd heard. All he could make out was a white shape. Indistinct.

"Hello?" He called in his head again. "What's she looking at? *Don't just fucking stand there! Help me!*"

The shape moved round him distantly – maddeningly silent, as he watched through the gap in his blindfold and turned and tilted his head as best he could – his heart beat drumming in his ears. In the midst of this mind numbing terror, a tiny part of his brain managed to retain a quiet, level headed and analytical view of the whole thing – a small, shrinking reserve perhaps best described as something like 'the eye of the storm'.

Goosebumps arose all over his naked upper body, despite the warmth radiating back from the vinyl under him. He knew by now whoever it was at his bedside was probably female – a woman, from the sound of the shoes. She was wearing white, as far as he could see. The most puzzling and maddening – and terrifying - part so far was that she hadn't said or done anything – other than to hover. Hovering meant trouble. Not saying anything meant trouble. Not helping meant trouble. ... He was in big, trouble.

She moved round to his head, until she was behind him where he could no longer see her, and stopped. His body was soaking wet with sweat, his muscles tense as he tugged ineffectually at his bonds. She wasn't going to help him, he realized – otherwise she already would have by now. The only thing that part of him wondered now was, how this was going to end?

He felt pressure on the blindfold, a tugging, and then the rough material was removed. The light was even more blinding now that he was getting a full dose of it. He blinked, squinting. Then he saw her, standing there, at the foot of his... bed – looking at him. The Nurse. It was then that he knew it was all over, or was going to be soon! It was all in the eyes. They were dark and black and soulless, framed perfectly against the white pallor of her expressionless face by their dark outline and long dark lashes and the dark curls of her head. They bored into him, unblinking, burning through his eyes and along his fraying synapses, to his unraveling mind, right into his very soul!

He couldn't speak, even if his mouth hadn't been restrained. She didn't speak, even though she was clearly unimpaired from doing so. He surveyed her features. Her lips were red and full, framed in a soft smile, which under the circumstances he found himself at a loss to use any word other than vacant to describe. The lights made her look harsh and intimidating, like a domme – well, how he would have imagined a domme to look. He wasn't the submissive type.

James Booth watched, mesmerized as the Nurse tilted her head almost theatrically, and produced a shiny scalpel in one dainty hand. Seeing his numbed expression, she proceeded to reach out to his left ankle and began to cut his pants away from that point. James raised his head to watch her automaton-like mechanical movements as she calmly and smoothly sliced through the material, not so much as nicking his skin even once, despite his involuntary jerks. She appeared to be in no hurry.

He noticed with dismay and mounting embarrassment as she worked her way up the inside of his trouser leg, that he had wet himself – a great wet patch had soaked the fabric of his track pants and had smeared on the ancient vinyl beneath. This scenario was taking on a hint of erotic thriller with a taste of psychotic horror! Why did she want him naked? Was she going to eat him? Was she actually going to eat him? His involuntary response immediately stifled and effectively cancelled by his intense resurgence of fear, and feeling even more naked than before, he watched helplessly as the Nurse removed the remains of the ruined garment – along with his underpants – and folded them into a neat bundle, before placing them precisely on top of an old gurney nearby, beside a shiny metal bedpan. James felt his Adam's apple bobbing nervously up and down. She had kept her eyes on him the whole time. Those eyes. Those. Terrible. Frightening. Empty. Black. Eyes.

Are they contacts? Does it matter? What the hell is this? Is this a prank? He wasn't getting married! He was pretty damned sure he wasn't! He didn't have any close friends here. *Enemies?* He swallowed again drily. He supposed anyone could have enemies. He couldn't think of any at the time, though. Least of all any with the resources to pull this off! All he could hear above the deafening silence in the room was his raging heart beating and his breathing. An occasional grunt or moan rebounded from his plugged mouth and escaped through his throat.

What the fuck does she want with me? His thoughts ran in an impotent mad circle of expletives and questions that had no answers. *How do I get outta this? Help! Fuck!*

It is at times like this, that people tend to ask what they feel are the 'important questions', where they become introspective and consider existential matters. They become concerned with things like who, where, why etc. Did James Booth have enemies? Did he have friends? Was this a prank? If it was, it was being taken a little far! Some say, if they are around afterwards, that their 'life flashed before their eyes'. It was currently what the people who had no 'afterwards' saw that occupied James Booth's thoughts.

Was Mr. Booth a lawyer or a bank clerk or a loving husband or a doting father? Was he a hero cop? Was he an airline pilot or a university professor? Was he a pastor at the local Baptist church? Did he donate to charities? Was he kind to women, old people or animals? Was he a bigot, a rapist, a murderer –

or was he a scam artist or a career criminal? Could he have been a generally nasty person? Someone, whom, one might be tempted to think might deserve this?

In a normal, ordinary every day story – say, one about butterflies and warm puppies – the reader celebrates the demise of the bad guy, the villain – and mourns the loss of the good guy... if there is really such a thing. They cheer when the bad guy takes a hit, and they cry when the hero falls – but isn't the main difference between a hero and a villain often only slightly a little more than timing? Or perhaps, perspective?

The typical readers of such humdrum tales – the sheep who accept the blue pill and swallow it with glee – would rejoice at the death of a bad person who did x, y, or z to deserve – at least in their minds – the fate they meet. To them it all makes sense – this is how it is supposed to go, after all – not so? Isn't it right and proper for the bad guys to meet a nasty, sticky end? No, dear reader – that would be far too mundane a scenario to apply here... and far too easy.

When dissecting a story, most people search for answers within the lines of pretty prose and philosophical ramblings. They look for meaning in the storyline, they look for the hand of Fate, the fingerprints of Destiny – sometimes for the shoeprints – or even, perhaps in his case – the tire-treads of Karma. They ask deep, meaningful emotive questions with – if ever answered correctly – life changing answers. *'What was it all about?' 'What was it for?'* And the old favorite: *'Why is this happening to me?'* And so on.

Without meaning, life is pretty pointless, isn't it? Without meaning, there is no point. They seek truth. But the question is: *'What is the truth?'* The truth, dear reader, is for armchair philosophers and possibly, for ministers of religion who deal with the abstract concepts of 'good' and 'evil' – which are often difficult to define and can be highly subjective in and of themselves. It could be pointed out that in this instance, the truth is five foot eight, black-eyed and dressed as a nurse... but perhaps it's best that we stick to facts in this case? And what are the facts?

James Booth was a man, a confused and terrified man – a naked man, in more ways than one – tied to a table in a deserted basement, facing... her.

The Nurse slowly tilted her head askance, still looking at him – seeming to savor every moment of his torment. Her lips parted slowly, almost hypnotically and mesmerized, he gawked as the teeth if they could be called that at all, were revealed. Framed by those lush red lips, they were starkly gray, tainted, and all of them sharp and vicious looking. Black gums dripped with equally black mucous which clung to them, that looked more like flecks of running motor oil than either blood or saliva – or any other bodily fluid that came to mind – dripping slowly from the upper row of teeth, across the maw down to the lower. What could only have been a tongue – mottled brown and purple in the blinding light of the ancient theater lights, pointy and slime covered – flicked and wriggled in the darkness between them. It dramatically stroked the sharp tips of the teeth in a theatric fashion, and played between the peaks and valleys. The pungent reek of decay emanating from it hit him like a blast of hot desert air, stinking like very old, very ripe death. It was right then that what was left of James Booth's hopes sank to the cold hard concrete floor. He knew this was no mere human being – twisted or otherwise – and his repository of expletives completely and utterly failed him.

Then she... IT ...closed its mouth and slowly turned and walked very deliberately to the gurney, stopping in front of the bedpan. Very quietly, with its back toward him, it put down the scalpel, reached into the bedpan and produced what looked like an old fashioned, rusty bone saw. This it placed onto the gurney, beside the bedpan and continued to produce more baffling and terrifying devices from its shiny fathomless depths.

Meanwhile, preparing himself for a rollercoaster ride into oblivion...and powerless to break free, James Booth's hands clamped around the edge of the base he lay upon, tightly, knuckles whitened. But wait... what was that? There was something small, loose, in the groove between the vinyl padded bed base and the corroded metal frame beneath his right hand. His eyes were locked onto the awful specter before him, which was producing mystery items from the depths of the bedpan like a magician pulling fluffy bunnies out of his magic hat, and lovingly caressing each one before putting it carefully down beside the others. His fingers rubbed up against the thing, feeling for some kind of recognizable object that could help him get out of this terrifying predicament.

A sudden sharp stabbing pain in his index finger told him all he needed to know. Carefully, he maneuvered the rusty scalpel blade around, his fingers quivering with urgency, panic and abject terror – careful to not drop it on the floor, since that would seal his doom faster than a slip on a tightrope with no safety net. Getting a grip on the thing wasn't easy, as the droplets of his blood on the rusty surface made it slippery and difficult to hold with the finger tips on one hand. Very carefully, he began to wiggle his hand in maddeningly tiny movements, slicing away at the strap pinning down his right wrist to the bed – while he watched, spell bound, as the Nurse carried on examining each medical instrument – or instrument of torture with morbid distraction. As the antique restraint clamping his wrist to the bed began to fray and loosen, his hopes began to soar!

Come on! Come on! Wiggle, wiggle. Almost through!

Just at that very moment, his right arm straining to cut away at the strap, his aching fingers fumbled the little blade and it slipped away! In frantic silence, he searched for it with his fingers. If it was out of reach, he was done!

I'm fucked! I'm dead! This is it! He thought.

A moment later, thankfully, he found it again in the same little furrow between the frame and the padding. Trying very hard to not release the sigh of relief he really wanted to, he carefully gripped the blade again and resumed the tedious process of cutting. The last strands frayed away and parted with a very faint snap. The Nurse was still stroking a toy – something that looked like a chest spreader – back toward him, as though the thing could actually purr. Very carefully, and as quickly as he could, he reached over with his aching numb right arm to pass the small blade to his still restrained left hand, before returning his right to the same position. The strap around his wrist, still tight, made it seem as though nothing had changed. Very carefully, he gripped the blade with the fingers of his left hand, cutting away at the strap. His mouth hurt – the ball gag thing was very definitely outstaying its welcome! *What kind of people would wear these things for fun?* he thought. In the meantime, he had lost focus on the Nurse – noting with sudden surprise that it wasn't at the gurney anymore. Where –

A sudden detection of the presence close by his right ear made him freeze. There was nothing metaphorical about the very real chill that ran up his spine. It was right there, leaning forward, craning over him, its face so close he could feel no warmth at all being reflected back at him. He listened very intently. He couldn't hear breathing! *Is it even alive? What is it?*

Those vacant black eyes moved – he couldn't see any irises or pupils – somehow the eyes reminded him of a rodent's – all solid color, black as night, but the surface of them moved towards him and held him in their gaze. This creature was, however, a lot more menacing and scary than any rodent he'd kept as a childhood pet. *Wiggle, wiggle. Just keep cutting.*

It sidled round the bed, high heels clicking faintly on the floor until it was at his right side, looking down at him like a microbe under a lens, squirming. *Just keep cutting! Keep cutting!* It slowly raised one hand, holding up what looked like something designed to saw through bone using two hands, before theatrically placing the cold metallic thing lightly on his chest, flat, and turning its head to enjoy his reaction.

Cut! Cut! Cut! Motherfucker! Mother-fucker! Moth-er-fuck-er! His frantic thoughts went as he surreptitiously sliced through the last strands holding his left wrist to the bed. He knew he would have to free his feet too, to have any realistic chance of escape – but one step at a time.

Considering how tired his wrists and fingers were from cutting, it surprised him how quickly and smoothly he was able to use them to seize his opportunity. The breastplate cutter was cold and heavy in his grasp, but when he grabbed it and swung it at his tormentor in one smooth movement, he was rewarded with the satisfying sensation of unbelievably sharp surgical steel slashing through clothing and the flesh beneath it!

The white figure stumbled backwards a few steps, seemingly injured and struggling! He sat up, and leaned forward to grapple with the bonds tying down his ankles! Now able to use his hands freely, he all but tore them loose in seconds! In the moments that followed, he struggled to his feet, dizzily lurching into the theater light assembly, sending the thing squeaking a few feet across the floor on its decrepit castors – looking like a surreal gothic nightmare. Light shifted, shadows moved, and – bone saw raised in his right hand – he whirled round and round trying to spot his adversary... but the Nurse had vanished!

There was blood – of a sort – on the floor a few feet away, where he'd seen it stumble. A black, sticky-looking ooze... but no creature! He paused to yank the god-awful gag thing free, and threw it across the chamber with disgust. As the sound of the ball bouncing across the distant concrete floor faded away, something touched on the naked skin of his shoulder. Reacting immediately, he saw what it was. Black. Dripping. He looked up.

"What the... " he breathed.

It was on the ceiling, mouth moving, grinning, not a voice or a whisper – more a raspy would-be voice – rising in deathly laughter. If he wasn't already so terrified, he would've screamed, but there was no time! The creature dropped on top of him, hands outstretched like claws, jaws open and yawning wide like a shark.

He side stepped as quickly as he could, the thing almost missing him as it descended – but dragging him down to the dusty floor by the legs! Kicking out and twisting, he slipped free from its grasp, and then with bravery which surprised even himself, he lunged forward and pounced on top of the creature, kneeing and punching it wherever he could get a shot in! He straddled the flailing hissing and squeaking thing as it bucked beneath him, face-down, like it was a demon-possessed horse, ignoring swipes from its claws as it tried to tear the flesh from his bones. His fists became a blur of force and motion as he poured his anger, outrage, fear and hate into the task. His head whirled as – screaming – he gripped the now mussed up and tousled black curls with both hands – and began slamming that horrid face into the unforgiving floor... again and again, and again! Black ooze marked the floor as he felt the skull beneath the nasty countenance crack and begin to give under his hands. He didn't stop until the white uniform – now completely smeared with grime, dust, black ooze and slime – went completely limp.

Exhausted, he sank back, sitting on his feet and on top of the still shapely rump of his fallen foe, breathing heavily, muscles quivering with relief, elation and disbelief. Feeling elated, he gave the aforementioned deceased rump a playful smack. Then he paused to think about what had just happened.

"What the fuck?" he breathed. Then, as the reality set in: *"What the fuck!"*

A movement caught his eye. Several fingers on its left hand were twitching, in what he thought were probably death throes. Wiping sweat from his face with one slime-smeared hand, while reaching onto the floor behind him for the fallen bone saw with the other which he brought down hard, cleanly severing the limb above the wrist with one blow.

Then, putting off the mounting urge to get the hell out of there as fast as his legs could carry him – momentarily absorbed in his morbid fascination, James Booth reached out towards its misshapen head, first moving the wisps of dead black hair out of the way with one hand, then after putting the blade down, with two. The Nurse's black hollow eyes were open, still staring vacantly, chillingly. The mouth was closed, full red lips impossibly intact and not bashed to smithereens as they should have been. Its face was smeared with the black blood it had been lying in that had pooled on the floor. The flesh was cold. Ice cold. *This is impossible!*

The thought ringing in his head like a church bell struck, the creature's head slowly began to move again. It turned toward him, expressionlessly, past the boundary of human anatomy – until it was facing back toward him at a complete one hundred and eighty degrees! The jagged, sharp mouth opened and the thing began hissing and squeaking as the head lunged toward him once more!

Screaming, more from shock than anger, he raised the blade again, and brought the instrument down sharply on its neck, severing the repulsive thing's head completely. Still shaking, as he watched the horrid head with the black curls bounce and roll in a surreal manner into the shadows, he struggled to his feet, dropped the weapon noisily on the floor and looked for the exit. Stumbling into the gurney, he ran past the headless corpse, his bare feet making wet slapping noises on the floor, like raw, wet pieces of meat smacking the top of a butcher's block, trailing messy footprints behind him.

After he made it through the door and into the maze of

underground corridors and rooms that spread beneath the old hospital, he ran and ran for all he was worth. Naked as he was, he didn't care. He felt free! Scared, shocked – but free. Triumphant too. Elated.

He didn't know what it was back there that had imprisoned him – or how it had caught him in the first place – and he still couldn't remember where he was and what he'd been doing before, but he was glad to be alive. Running felt good! And as the dark shadows of darkened doorways and openings flashed past in the near darkness, he didn't care how he was going to explain being naked and drenched in whatever it was... or his bruised and swollen knuckles, to anyone who asked. Alone in the dark with his thoughts, running in the pale light from isolated and flickering light fittings, the only sound he could hear was his breathing and his pounding footsteps as they echoed into the void...

***

James Booth's eyes flickered open. The lights were blinding. They were hot too, not like modern lights at all. They were blazing, almost singing him through the gaps in the broken lens covers. He struggled through the confusion. He remembered the car accident. It was night time, he... *wait*! There was something awfully familiar about this...

***

What do you think, dear reader? Did James Booth deserve to be in the situation in which he found himself? What evil could he have done to deserve it? Or what good? Was he – or was he not – a 'good guy'? Perhaps he was neither? Perhaps a little bit of both, as we all are? In the end, either option is really quite irrelevant.

The fact is that any one of us could be a James Booth. Any one. And that – for me at least – is the true essence of the horror in *horror*.

Here it is, dear reader, where we part ways and leave the horrible halls of this decrepit dungeon, which echoes with the resounding cries of the doomed, and the faint clicks of the heels of the damned... And while this endless night drags on, as it always does, the city slumbers its usual restless, blissfully ignorant slumber – and if you listen very carefully, there is the faint sound of distant screaming.

Sweet dreams.

(About **Christina Engela**: While Christina might not be the only writer – or even the only sci-fi writer from South Africa - she is certainly the most authentic, eccentric and unique sci-fi/fantasy/horror writer to originate from that country! This is not just because of the characters or settings she creates, or the unique situations she imagines, but also because of her life experiences, her unusual outlook on life – and the strange and often wacky things she notices in the world around her – and of course, her quirky sense of humor! In her fiction, she creates believable characters, and spins gripping tales that transport her readers to distant worlds, becoming absorbed in their lives and adventures! Christina is the proud owner of a warped sense of humor, and it shows in her writing – and also typically in ordinary conversation! She writes in the science-fiction/fantasy/horror genre, and has already published more than twenty titles in three series – and others, including a children's book about bullying. Christina has a lot of diverse life-experience to draw upon in her writing, having been a soldier with the South African Army for seventeen years – with all the diverse experience and challenging situations such service invariably brings. People often misjudge and underestimate her, usually to their peril).

COINS

by Richard Barr

There was something therapeutic about it, Colm thought. They felt cool under his fingertips. Cool and smooth. He imagined he was running his hand along a riverbed, the bumpy path of pebbles and stones underneath, his fingers rising and falling against them.

A boy and his granny watched as the coins fell from Colm's large jar. The jar was embossed with a procession of cartoon people clutching to their chests implausibly enormous wads of cash.

Colm turned the jar as all his coins poured out, looking to see if this very wealthy grouping would arrive somewhere or, even, be met by some comeuppance.

Colm noticed the boy watching. "They just walk around and around, never ending. I'd say that's the worst fate of all, eh?"

"Probably," replied the boy.

Colm held his hand out, placed it under the falling coins, let them all tumble between his fingers into the tray below.

"It feels like water," he said.

"Funny water," said the boy.

"Funny money?" asked the granny.

"Not at all," said Colm, turning the jar up.

He turned his back on the pair, and, facing the machine, closed his eyes. Momentarily, everything quietened at once and all he was aware of was the rush of blood through his head.

The boy spoke. "How does it work?"

"I don't know," said Colm. "I come here every month and empty my coins into it. I tip the tray up," he said, lifting the tray, "the coins disappear. After they're counted, it prints you out a ticket that says what it all amounts to."

"That's convenient," said the granny.

"Yes," said Colm. "You take this ticket and trade it in at the counter."

The noisy process of the coin sorting began. The tossing and clattering and bashing became louder and soon drowned out the noise of the supermarket. It sounded as if a whole lot of people were building some deadly and horrific weapon.

"How much do you think's there?" shouted the granny.

"Usually, it'll be around a tenner," Colm shouted back. "This month I've had cause to collect up a lot more change, won't get into why, so I'm expecting a higher total."

The boy stared at the ticket dispenser. "I wonder," he shouted, "if a savant could make a reasonable guesstimate on the total amount in there just by the sound of it all alone?"

"I might give this gizmo a go myself," said the granny.

"A great piece of technology," said Colm, his eyes, with theirs, fixed on the ticket dispenser.

Gradually, the cacophony slowed and stopped, giving way to the whirr of the ticket machine, which flashed red then green.

"Please, please, please," whispered Colm, clenching and unclenching his fists.

The boy and his granny looked at him and then back at the dispenser. Immediately, they felt a great but inexplicable sense of solidarity with Colm. What emerged from that dispenser, what it all came to, suddenly, for them also, took on a great and deep significance.

(**Richard Barr** lives and works in County Antrim, Northern Ireland. He's had several short works appearing in the last year published in *The Luminary* and *The Big Issue,* and also in comic-book anthologies *Courageous Mayhem* and *Hold The Phones, It's Alex Jones.* He received a 'Very Honourable Mention' in the 'Weekend Writing Challenge' offered by The Other Publishing Company. Previously, his screenplay, *A Place for Everything,* made the final round of Digital Shorts, a joint project between the BBC and Northern Ireland Screen. Richard also provided the concept for the novel *Axel America and the U.S. Election Race* and contributed to *Gruesome Grotesques Volume 2: Vampires, Werewolves and Other Beautiful Monsters* and *Gruesome Grotesques Volume 3: Codex Gigas [Tales of the Occult]*).

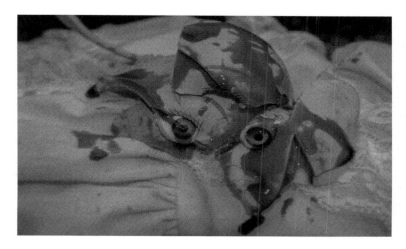

MR HARDDON AND THE TURTLEY AWESOME ADVENTURE

by Karina Sims

The young woman put her coffee on the table then parted the curtains. Outside it was gray and early, the birds sang. She drank her coffee and watched a dog trot up the street.

Her eyes were tired and caught on the neighbor's fence. *I GOT A DONKEY KONG DONG* was painted in big blue letters across the street. Empty cans of Krylon laid around the mail box.

She looked at her wedding ring, paused and adjusted it. She rubbed her finger then sipped coffee and looked back out the window.

***

Across town, Tyson Oliver was just waking up. His arms swung at the four-thirty alarm, his fingers hit the snooze button twice before getting up. He didn't take a shower and he didn't brush his teeth. He didn't even put on underwear. Just a t-shirt and some overalls, some boots and a hat. He stood six feet two inches and was thick as a bowl of oatmeal. His hair was short and red and stuck out all over the place. His face wasn't particularly handsome, and he was pale. But his height and build often brought him women, who *always* brought him problems.

Today he stepped quietly into the hall of the boarding house. He was renting a room, paying eighty dollars a week. The moment she pocketed his money, the landlady had stuck her finger in his chest and looked him so hard in the eyes, it reminded him of the nuns who thrashed schoolboys. She said, "Look here, *I'm* Ms. McQuaid! I'm the *law* here."

She was old and ugly from the inside out. "No *women*, no *drinking*. No laying around! Do you have a *job*?"

It took a moment, but he swallowed his pride and nodded. "Yes, ma'am."

She was visibly taken back by his manners and soft tone. She raised her eyebrows, her fingers rubbed and tugged at the crucifix dangling between her two sagging breasts. "Oh…" She trailed off into an inaudible mutter.

He said, "Do you have a TV?"

She had shaken her head, eyes aimed at the floor. As she turned and walked away, Tyson caught, "Yes, but the cable is out. We're waiting for the repair man."

He had then locked his door and she shuffled up the stairs, mumbling to herself.

This morning, the sky and the clouds stirred about, dull and lifeless, like gray syrup. Tyson opened the front door and trotted down a dozen lumber steps onto the street. Cold air bit the tip of his nose and ate at the skin around his nostrils. He wiped his chin with his bare arm then climbed into his truck. The engine came to life with Creedance Clearwater Revival blasting through the speakers. He didn't turn it down. He reached over and pulled on a jean jacket and started driving.

He drummed his fingers on the steering wheel and sang, "*It ain't me! It aain't mee!*"

***

The young woman sighed. She stood and looked at the clock. It was nearly five AM. Her mug was empty, she left it there on the table and moved slowly into the living room. She turned on the TV at the moment the front door opened. She didn't hear it.

Heavy boots dropped to the floor and Tyson Oliver slipped quietly down the hall. The young woman was watching television when he stepped into the room.

He said, "What's happening?"

Her eyes didn't leave the screen. "You're late. I'll tell you during commercials."

He signed and sat down on the opposite end of the couch. He rubbed his eyes and asked for coffee.

She said, "Get it yourself."

He did, during a commercial break and she followed him into the kitchen.

She said, "The bald guy with all the guns is plotting to take over China Town."

Tyson filled the kettle and turned on the stove. He stepped into the dining room, put his hands on his hips and looked out the window, frowning at the fence. He said, "Can we stop playing games, Laquisha? Can we talk about Ray? What's going on?"

She crossed her arms, rolled her eyes and scoffed all at once. She said, "Maybe *you* could try talking to your son for once instead of *me* being the only one here for him *and* I got to *work*!"

Tyson was silent. He rested against the table and the kettle screamed. He picked up the mug she had left earlier and carried it into the kitchen. He poured his coffee into it and sipped quietly.

She said, "You could've just used a clean one, you know."

He shrugged. "I know how much you hate doing dishes."

Her eyes squinted. "What does *that* mean?"

In the other room, the show came back on and the two of them sat on the couch, far away from one another.

They sat in silence until the commercials. Laquisha muted the TV and turned to Tyson. "What do you think?"

"I think our son is an idiot for watching this crap. Jesus... so, *these* are his idols?" He took off his jacket and folded it in his lap. "What kind of maniac sees something on TV and goes and sprays it all over the neighbor's fence?"

She bolted to attention. "*That* could have been *anybody*! Nobody's proved it was, Ray! Don't put that on him! You can't blame him for that without any damn *proof*!"

Tyson shook his head, "It was, Ray. I know it was Ray. In any case, I don't want him watching this show at all."

Laquisha nodded and unfolded her arms. She sat on her hands and looked at the carpet.

Tyson checked the time. "Why... why is this show even on right now? It's way too early. No teenager is even awake right now."

She muted the TV. "After every new episode, re-runs play until six AM."

"Oh." He stood up, stretched and put his jacket back on. "I've got to get to work. Thanks for having me over. Say hi to

Robbie for me will you?"

"He isn't here."

"Oh! Is he going for husband of the year?"

She gripped her ring and rubbed her finger. "Shut up."

"How long is he gone for this time?"

She turned her back and moved into the kitchen. Tyson followed after her. "Does he still have two phones?"

She grabbed the mug out of his hands and threw it at him. She missed. Coffee stained the rug and splattered all over the TV. She screamed *"Get out of my house!"*

He put his fist through a cabinet. "This is *my* fucking house!" He grabbed his boots and carried them out the door with him. He put them on as he walked toward the truck. Laquisha came out onto the step, "Don't ever fucking come back here!"

He stopped in his tracks and turned around. His shoulders felt heavy and he was wiping his eyes. "What kind of man leaves his pregnant wife at home, alone all the time?"

"Mind your *own damn* business, Tyson! I'm only two months pregnant, Robbie doesn't have to be here every moment of the day! Tyson, you start being a better father to *your* son; and stop worrying about what the fuck Robbie is doing!"

She slammed the door and went back into the living room. The television was dripping with coffee. She picked up the remote and swore. The screen went green, glitched then shut off.

***

By ten-thirty, Ms. McQuaid stood on the lumber steps of her boarding house, wringing her hands. She was waiting for a man from the cable company and he was forty-five minutes late. She had called three times in the past half hour and, the third time, they let the phone ring and didn't even pick up. But the woman on the other line *had* assured her many times during both conversations that *yes*, someone *was* coming and to wait patiently until they arrive. She said they were experiencing a high volume of calls in the area, then she thanked Ms. McQuaid for being a customer and hung up.

By eleven forty-five, Ms. McQuaid sat on her lumber steps and peeled potatoes. A van with ladders on the roof parked on the street in front of the house. A thin, ugly man with horse teeth got out of the truck and stood six feet eleven inches into the sky. Around his shoulder was a bag, filled to pop with tools.

He was a *tower* of a man, which made his ugliness all the more disappointing. Nobody he knew would ever breathe a word but, they all thought exactly the same thing as Ms. McQuaid as she stood to greet him. '*My God*, what a waste of an incredible frame.'

His eyes were squinty and he fumbled with his glasses as he greeted her. "Good morning, Missus! I'm Chip, are you having trouble with the cable?"

She wiped his smile away with her posture. She put one hand on her hip and stuck the other out at him, pointing a bent up and withered finger like a tiny sword she could cut him with. "Look at your damn *clipboard*! It's not *Missus* it's *Miss*! And it's *not* morning! It's *afternoon* and you're *late*!"

Chip looked at his watch then back at her. He shifted the bag beneath his arm. He was smiling again. "Take me to the trouble, will you?"

Ms. McQuaid sucked her lips and hissed, "*This* way." She

stomped her feet and led him upstairs.

Tyson Oliver met them on the second floor. He was opening the door to his room, which was filled with liquor bottles. He blocked the doorway with his massive frame and nodded in greeting. "Good afternoon, McQuaid."

Chip stepped forward, extending a skinny arm with long fingers, he shook Tyson's hand and said, "I'm Chip, the cable guy! What's your name, buddy?"

Tyson shook his hand. "What happened to the cable?"

Chip put a hand in his pocket and cleared his throat. He adjusted the strap of his bag. "Knocked off. All of them, half a dozen block around here..." he clapped his hands together, the sound was loud, and snapped through the hallway and down the staircase. "...slapped right off the rooftops."

Tyson raised his eyebrows, he looked gobsmacked, staring back and forth at Chip at Ms. McQuaid. He stuttered, "Who's done this?"

She tugged the crucifix around her neck and stared into nothing, for only a moment. She snapped back, as if making up her mind. She said, "Kids. Kids did it."

Chip pushed his glasses up and smiled, "We aren't at liberty to say but between buddies..." He leaned. "It *was* kids."

Tyson's heart sank into his chest. Chip and Ms. McQuaid went upstairs.

In the attic, Chip popped his head around the window. Immediately upon entering, Ms. McQuaid's head was pounding. Dust made her sick.

Chip stepped back from the window sill and brushed at his clothes. "Yup. I see the trouble here. Your antenna has been knocked clean off the roof."

She sat on a wooden crate next to a bird cage and sneezed. "How can you tell the antenna's been knocked off? You didn't even look at it!" She dug in her shirt and came out with a handkerchief. She wiped her nose and sneezed again.

He said, "I saw it knocked off, on the drive over."

She slapped her knees and stood up. "Why the *hell* did you have me come up here then?" She mumbled with hubris and stomped angrily down the pull-out staircase.

***

At three PM, Ray Oliver was carving *EAT SHIT* into the desk in front of him. His teacher, Mr. Harddon, entered the room in a flourish, throwing the door open behind him. He slipped both thumbs and index fingers around his hips, leaving the other ones free to dance as he spoke. He stood like a queer and glared at Ray digging *SHIT* out on the desk with a knife.

Mr. Harddon cleared his throat with a chirp. "You can go home, Ray." Ray rose his head but lowered it again when he saw the intensity in Mr. Harddon's glare. "But, I'm calling your mother this evening. I've had enough of this horse poop behavior of yours."

He said this in a way that made Ray feel Mr. Harddon was trying to get a reaction out of him.

He didn't say anything and allowed the room to fall to silence. After a long minute of Mr. Harddon standing like a queer and staring at Ray, he repeated. "You can go home now."

Ray nodded and put his backpack on his lap. He said, "Can I go out the window?"

Without moving a muscle or breaking his stare, Mr.

Harddon said, "Yes. You can leave through the window." Then he left the room and didn't close the door.

Ray slid out the window, tearing his backpack.

***

Before dinner, Ms. McQuaid liked tuning the radio into soft listening. Drawing a bath while the food cooled on the table was absolutely necessary for her well being. Everyday of her adult life, she did this. Today was no different than any other day except today, when she climbed into the water and felt around for the soap, the word *CUNT* rose up through the water, in the white letters.

She blinked, then gasped. She felt her heart stop beating as black reptile eye broke above the water, the ugly green head of a tiny snapping turtle bobbed and hissed at her.

CUNT written in big white letters on it's shell. She screamed and thrashed the little beast out of the tub. She looked in horror at the floor. Dozens of tiny snapping turtles with swear words written on them in white marker, shuffled and scratched across the tile. One said *PUSSY*. Another said *FUCK*. In the corner by the door, two huddled together and spelled *DICK FART*.

***

Ray stood across the street from his house, laughing at the neighbor's fence. Tyson had come back over and installed a new TV for Laquisha. He saw Ray through the front window. The telephone rang, Laquisha answered it as Tyson stepped out the door.

Ray saw him coming and waved him over, "Hey, dad! You seen this?" He was still laughing.

Tyson yelled "*Yeah*, you sure as hell I did, *get in the*

goddamn house, Ray! You're grounded!"

Ray stepped back, "What?"

Tyson grabbed his arm. "I know it was *you*! I saw that damn graffiti gang show you love so much. It's garbage. You're grounded! Get in the house!"

Laquisha hung up the phone as Ray and Tyson came through the door. "What's this about you vandalizing teacher property?"

Tyson let go of his arm and grabbed Ray's backpack. "Did you rip *this*? This was *brand* new!"

Ray stomped his foot and punched the fridge. Tyson shouted, "Don't punch shit when you're angry!"

Ray shouted then covered his head. "Will you let me *talk*? I *didn't* vandalize anything!"

Tyson began to speak but Laquisha held up her hand, "Go ahead, son. Tell us what happened. I believe you." She glared angrily from the side at Tyson, then smiled warmly at Ray. "You take as much time as you need to, baby. I'm listening."

He told the truth, but he kept his head down the whole time. "At lunch, I put some tape over one of the D's on Mr. Harddon's name plaque that's on his classroom window."

Laquisha screwed up her face. "What? Why?"

Ray stumbled on his words. "Because, it's um, it's really funny."

Laquisha started smiling but, she turned around for a moment and when she turned back around she was frowning again, "Okay well, you go upstairs now and let me talk to your father."

"Am I grounded?"

She waved at him to hurry up and leave the room. "No, you *ain't* grounded. You go to bed now."

"It's six o'clock!"

"I'll bring you dinner. Go to bed now."

Tyson started, "He's still grounded if..."

Laquisha stomped her foot, "YOU AIN'T GROUNDED, RAY! *GO TO BED!*"

Ray left the room and went upstairs. Tyson was crossing his arms and shaking his head, ready to burst, when there was a knock at the door.

He and Laquisha looked at each other. "Who could that be?"

He looked in the mirror and fixed his hair, then he opened the door.

It was Chip, the repair man from Ms. McQuaid's building. He was smiling. "Your cables out."

Two dogs trotted up the street, barking. Tyson watched the street lamps light up in rows. He said, "No it's not. I've been watching TV all night."

He smiled. "Are you sure?"

"I'm watching *The Karate Kid*. The old one. Not the new dumb one. I hate Jaden Smith and I think his dad sucks."

Laquisha touched his arm. "I'll check." She came back a minute later. "It's out."

"What!?" Tyson stomped into the living room and pushed

every button on the remote. The cable *was* out. He gripped the remote tightly in his fist and looked at the ceiling. *Ray,* he thought, *that little shit.*

Laquisha let Chip in the house. He smiled, "Can I go to the attic?" She nodded, pointed Chip to the stairs then joined Tyson in the living room.

She crossed her arms and stood beside him. His voice my heavy and held back. "Would you have a word with Ray please?"

She slapped his arm. "Oh hush. Ray didn't have anything to do with this mess.

He sighed and hung his head. He rubbed his eyes and tried to stay calm. "*Laquisha* would you please speak to our son about this?"

She sighed too. "This is bullshit." She left the room and walked quickly upstairs. She knocked on her son's door, not waiting for him to answer, she opened it. He was sitting at his desk doing homework.

She stopped dead in her tracks. "Oh God." She clapped her hands to her face.

Ray smiled, "What?"

She shook her head, grinning ear to ear. "Doing your *homework*!? My angel from heaven. I love you so *much*! Come here. Come hug your momma." She waved him over and they stood there holding each other, soul to soul, until loud thumps from the attic ruined the moment.

"The hell...?" Laquisha's head left her son's shoulder. They watched the cable antenna fall past the window. It crashed onto the lawn.

There were footsteps, then a cracking sound and Chip's giant, gangly body flew off the roof. His limbs, long and extended, he looked like a spider being dropped out of a jar. One of his weird hands gripped onto the ledge, causing his massive frame to collide with Ray's window, which shattered on impact, and broke the blinds.

As he hung there, he twisted his face like monster. His eyes were round and wild. Turtles crawled through his hair, biting his face. They wriggled in his clothes and spilled out of the bag around his shoulder. They fell to the ground with things like *POO* and *ASS* written on their back.

One of his teeth had been knocked out. He laughed like a maniac and spat blood when he spoke. "It's time to shell-ebrate!" A turtle bit him in the eye and he fell to the ground.

They ran outside but Chip was gone.

Turtles with *AIDS* and *COCK* crawled across the lawn.

Tyson called the cable company. He was immediately put through to management but remained on hold for several minutes. When they finally answered, and Tyson told them about what had happened he was put back on hold for more minutes. When he was taken off hold, he spoke to a different person who gruffly explained to him that Chip was actually Edmond Forring, who happened to be the son of the mayor. Edmond has mental problems and acts up from time to time but for the most part is a good citizen and the town's people tolerate him. Edmond does not work for the cable company and his actions of destroying people's cable antennas and filling their homes with reptiles has absolutely nothing to do with the company or their standards of customer service. They told Tyson to call in the morning, they said they would send someone straight out for the cable.

Tyson shook his head and looked out the window. "But,

what about all these damn *turtles*?”

“We don’t deal with turtles, sir. That’s not our problem that you keep turtles.” The voice on the other line was silent for a moment. Then a slight crackle in the line, a stifled laugh. “Hate...hate to leave you in a *turtle disaster,* sir but um...” The voice broke into wild laughter then hung up.

Tyson stood outside, holding the phone gone to dial tone. *EAT SHIT* stumbled together under the porch lights.

(**Karina Sims** is an artist and author from British Columbia, Canada. She writes scripts for indie films and short stories for various magazines and horror anthologies. Her first novel was *Sinners Circle*. She loves cats and Kurt Cobain).

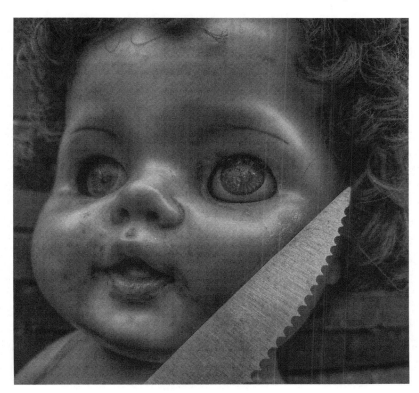

THE ENTIRE *GRUESOME GROTESQUES* INTERNATIONAL ANTHOLOGY SERIES SO FAR IS CURRENTLY ON SALE FROM AMAZON AND FORBIDDEN PLANET, BELFAST:

ASIAN MONSTER KINGS

FROM *GOJIRA* (1954) TO *THE HOST* (2006): SOCIAL AND POLITICAL COMMENTARY IN KAIJU CINEMA

by Nathan Waring

(Picture copyright of Toho Film Co. Ltd).

The following piece is an exploration of Kaiju (Giant Monster) Cinema, and its tradition of commenting on contemporary political and societal anxieties. The idea for the writing of this struck me upon viewing *The Host* (2006) in a Cinema of Modernity university class, where I noticed some striking similarities between the film and other films in the Kaiju Genre, most notably with the original *Gojira,* or *Godzilla,* (1954)

In my research, I used various books and sources of information, including books on Kaiju Cinema, such as *The Kaiju Film: A Critical Study of Cinema's Biggest Monsters* (2016), and books on Korean Cinema, such as *The South Korean Film Renaissance: Local Hitmakers/Global Provocateurs* (2010). I also immersed myself with Kaiju Cinema, and watched many genre classics such as *King Kong* (1933), *Gojira, The Return of Godzilla* (1984), *The Host* and *Godzilla* (2014).

The crux of this examination is the idea that the Kaiju genre uses the monsters and narratives in their films to explore cultural anxieties of the societies they are released to. I do this by first by analysing *Gojira,* which highlighted the societal fears of nuclear war and contamination that were widespread in the Japanese society the film was first shown to in 1954. I then go on to discuss how the Kaiju films that followed continued this tradition of commenting on societal fears, such as the film *Mothra* (1961) which tackled environmental concerns, followed by an overview of Korean Kaiju Cinema. This leads in to a discussion of *The Host,* which, like *Gojira* and various other Kaiju films before it, debates contemporary societal anxieties, such as fears about the SARS virus and criticism of both the Korean and American governments.

It is my hope that anyone reading this will come away with a better understanding of Kaiju Cinema, perhaps even making them re-evaluate their preconceived notions about the genre.

From perhaps the beginning of human storytelling, concepts

such as giant monsters and destructive beasts have remained a constant, with the most prominent examples being the Leviathan of Biblical mythology, the Kraken of Norse legend and, most notably, the tales of dragons which proliferated during the Medieval age. These fantastical creatures were often representations of contemporary fears, such as the Kraken representing the fear of being lost at sea or dragons being viewed as the representations of Hell and demons of European religious lore. With the advent of film technology, these types of stories were given a new avenue which not only allowed them to tell a story involving enormous creatures, but also gave the storytellers the chance to display their monsters visually, with one of the earliest examples being *The Ghost of Slumber Mountain* (1918), which used stop-motion animation techniques to create its dinosaurian stars. *The Ghost of Slumber Mountain* would be followed up seven years later with *The Lost World* (1925), the first adaptation of Sir Arthur Conan Doyle's classic 1912 novel, which greatly improved on the use of stop-motion. In 1933, the concept of a giant film monster would become fully realised in the cultural consciousness with the release of *King Kong* (1933), which authors Sean Rhoads and Brooke McCorkle have described as 'one of the first and most influential monster movies, *King Kong* represents a zenith of giant monster cinema'. *King Kong* was different to earlier giant monster films as it portrayed the titular monster in a sympathetic light, much like the characterisation of Boris Karloff's monster in James Whale's seminal *Frankenstein* (1931), as the film 'critiqued the exploitative horrors of the human world – particularly the deprivations of the Great Depression – and Kong himself is less of a monster to be feared than a creature to be pitied' (McCorkle and Rhoads, 2018). *King Kong* is often cited as the true beginning of the giant monster movie genre, as it addressed 'themes that would reverberate throughout later monster movies, most notably a tension between nature and humanity (or perhaps more accurately human science and technology)' (McCorkle and Rhoads, 2018). This notion would later become one of the many themes of the most well known subgenre of giant monster cinema: Kaiju.

Kaiju (roughly translated to 'strange beast' in English) Cinema can trace its genre ancestry back to American productions like *King Kong* (1933) and *The Beast From 20,000 Fathoms* (1953), films which allowed for the producers at Toho Studios in Tokyo to see 'the potential for the monster cinema genre in Japan' (McCorkle and Rhoads, 2018), eventually leading to the creation of perhaps the most well known monster in all of popular culture with the Japanese release of *Gojira* (Godzilla) in 1954. *Gojira* was, pun intended, a Godzilla-sized success in both its native country and around the world, where it was released in an Americanized version that changed the original story by including scenes featuring veteran American actor Raymond Burr. The film would spark a worldwide boom in giant monster cinema that is still in place today with such releases as *Cloverfield* (2008) and *Pacific Rim* (2013), and also saw the beginning of the *Godzilla* franchise that so far spans thirty one films, two television series and a plethora of merchandise, and has been described as one of the earliest examples of the 'cinematic universe' (a series of loosely connected films that tell one over-arching story), a franchise model which would find enormous success over fifty years later with the *Marvel Cinematic Universe* (2008 onwards). The impact of the original Godzilla on the cultural zeitgeist is immeasurable and as 'a result, even though films like *King Kong* (1933) existed long before Godzilla first waded ashore, the idea of a giant creature wending its way through a city, either casually or destructively, is a strictly Japanese phenomenon' (Barr, 2016). Much like the earliest monster stories and *Kong* before it, *Gojira* uses its titular monster to represent contemporary societal fears, in this case the memory of the Second World War and the impact of nuclear testing. Much of Kaiju cinema explores these themes as well as many others, and typically they will comment on the fears and anxieties of the societies they are released to, with arguably the best modern example being the South Korean film *The Host* (2006).

In order to fully analyse the themes present in *Gojira,* it is important to contextualize the film within the view point of the society it was released to in 1954. Having been released only two years after the Allied Occupation of Japan (1945-1952) and a mere nine years after the atomic bombings of 1945, 'Gojira replays the horrors of nuclear war for the only country to experience atomic attack' as Godzilla's final attack on Tokyo 'turns the city into a blazing inferno generated by the creature's atomic breath that cannot help but recall the destruction wrought on Hiroshima and Nagasaki less than a decade before' (Grant, 2013). The film's director, Ishiro Honda, had served in China during World War II, and upon his return to his native land witnessed first-hand the devastation of Hiroshima, as well as the destruction caused by the saturation bombing of Tokyo and the effects of radiation sickness upon the population, all of which would influence his direction of Gojira and it is 'no surprise therefore that Godzilla...is both a thinly disguised metaphor for historical trauma and a warning against its repetition' (Balmain, 2008). Even the design of Godzilla himself can be said to evoke the anxieties of the war weary Japanese society of the 1950s, as one of the first designs had 'a mushroom-like head, to bring to mind the cloud of an atomic explosion' (Brown, 2012), while the creature's final design 'featured alligator-textured skin that resembled the keloid scars prevalent among survivors of the atomic bombings' (McCorkle and Rhoads, 2018). The film also draws inspiration from events that happened in the year of its release, as the opening sequence featuring Godzilla's destruction of a Japanese fishing boat harkens back to the nuclear contamination of the crew of the Daigo Fukuryu Maru (roughly translated to The Lucky Dragon) due to the fallout of the testing of the Castle Bravo thermonuclear weapon by the American military at Bikini Atoll, an event that would be fresh in the memory of the film's intended audience.

Themes of anti-Americanism are also prevalent in the film, as 'American nuclear testing created Godzilla' and, much like the American campaign in the Pacific conflict, 'he sinks several Japanese ships and decimates Tokyo' (McCorkle and Rhoads, 2018). These ideals are encapsulated in the film's climax when Dr. Serizawa uses his deadly weapon, known as the 'oxygen destroyer', to finally kill Godzilla (despite the protestations of the film's main character, Professor Yamane), alluding to the notion that while 'American science inadvertently creates Godzilla, it is a Japanese scientist who defeats Godzilla and saves the Japanese from immanent destruction' (McCorkle and Rhoads, 2018). The fact that Serizawa commits suicide so that the secrets of his weapon would die with him is perhaps suggesting that, unlike the American military, the Japanese would not commit the same atrocities perpetrated on Hiroshima and Nagasaki, as the 'sacrificial hero is an important mechanism through which traditional identity is restored in the face of encroaching Westernization' (Balmain, 2008). All of the issues discussed by the film would have hit its Japanese audience particularly hard as they touched upon the fears and anxieties of Japanese society at the time, while also imbuing the audience with trepidation in regards to the future as in the film's 'final shots...humanity's apparent victory is qualified as Yamane wonders whether the continued testing of nuclear weapons will unleash further mutated monsters upon the world' (Grant, 2013).

(Picture copyright of Toho Film Co. Ltd).

Indeed it would, as the success of *Gojira* would lead to a flourishing of Kaiju cinema both in Japan and around the world, a lot of which would also deal with the issues of their time. *Mothra* (1961), which featured a gigantic female moth as its titular creature, was different to *Gojira* in that the monster was the hero of the story, but no less culturally significant as Mothra represents 'both nature and the feminine. She is a monstrous symbol at odds with rapid post-war industrialization and the greedy pursuit of capital' (McCorkle and Rhoads, 2018), themes which would be further emphasised with Mothra's debut in the Godzilla series in 1964's *Mothra vs. Godzilla,* as well as in Mothra's subsequent film appearances. The Godzilla series itself would also see a great variation of themes, such as *Godzilla vs. Hedorah* (1971) which 'shifted the focus of the Godzilla franchise from nuclear fears to the crippling toil of rapid industrialization and its toxic pollution' (McCorkle and Rhoads, 2018), or *The Return of Godzilla* (1984), a reboot of the series that touched upon many of the same themes of the original *Gojira* 'while expanding on the issue to address peaceful nuclear power as well as saber-rattling between the superpowers in the late Cold War' (McCorkle and Rhoads, 2018).

(Picture copyright of Toho Company).

However, Kaiju films with political and social agendas would not be limited to Japan, as Korea also has a rich tradition of politically charged Kaiju cinema as the '1960s saw the emergence of the Korean giant monster movie, an obvious imitation of the diakaiju cycle that began with Ishiro Honda's truly iconic Godzilla' (Martin, 2013). The earliest example of a Korean kaiju film is *Taekoeso Yongary* (titled *Yongary: Monster from the Deep* in English speaking markets) from 1967, which contained scenes of civilians fleeing and evacuating from the monster's destructive path that were reminiscent of the real scenes of civilians fleeing the Korean War a decade and a half earlier. Similarly, North Korea would create its own 'ideologically specific giant monster movies, most notoriously with *Pulgasari*' in 1985, whose monster 'serves as a vivid propagandist metaphor for the exploitation of the proletariat' (Martin, 2013), although the horrific story behind the film (Kim Jong-Il had kidnapped South Korean director Shin Sang-ok in order to direct the film) somewhat negates its significance. Korean Kaiju cinema would reach its peak in 2006 with the release of Joon-ho Bong's monster masterpiece, *The Host,* which, like *Gojira* and many other Kaiju films before it, commented on the fears and anxieties of its target audience.

(Picture copyright of Showbox Entertainment/Chungeorahm Film).

The anti-American stance of *Gojira* is recreated as one of the most prominent themes of *The Host,* as the film begins with a prologue to the film's main story that shows an American military pathologist ignoring safety protocol by dumping large quantities of formaldehyde down the drain, which goes directly into Seoul's Han River and leads to the creation of the film's monster, and thus 'the film begins immediately addressing the United States military presence in Korea' (Grant, 2013). As was the case with *Gojira,* Bong draws inspiration from reality for his monster story, as 'Bong based his film on the true story of Albert McFarland' (Choi, 2010), an American civilian who worked at the morgue in a US military base in South Korea and, like the character in the film, dumped dangerous chemicals down the drain. This anti-American sentiment is seen throughout the film, most notably in the film's portrayal of the American government as 'unconcerned about its actions, as reflected in the closing sequence in which an American official regrets the "miscommunication" that led to the pollution" (Barr, 2016) and the creation of the monster itself. Adding to this is the American's use of the chemical known as Agent Yellow, a clear allusion to the Agent Orange chemical used in the Vietnam War, to combat the monster despite 'the objections of the South Korean people', which serves to paint 'the picture of the American military as boorish, ungrateful and uncaring' (Barr, 2016). This emphasis on the American presence in South Korea, as well as its interference in Korean affairs, would have been viewed by many of the film's Korean audience as echoing their own opinions on the matter, leading film critic Peter Bradshaw (in his review of the film for *The Guardian* newspaper) to muse: 'Could it be that the Americans, accustomed to treating South Korea as a buffer zone against Kim Jong Il's rogue state to the north, are the real aliens, the real monsters?' (Bradshaw, 2006). The film also does not shy away from criticising the Korean government as well, as the Park family (the main characters of the film) 'must also overcome the bureaucratic obstacles and outright hostility of the government, which deliberately establishes a false cover story about a virus and quarantines everyone' (Grant, 2013), alluding to the idea that the Parks, along with Korean society in general, was 'so used to getting trampled on by the state that a two-ton monstroid doesn't make much of a difference' (Crook, 2006).

Another important theme of *The Host,* and one which perhaps best plays into the anxieties of Korean society, and Asian society in general, is the film's depiction of government procedural action to prevent the spread of disease. In the film, both the American and Korean governments proliferate a cover story to hide the existence of the monster, saying that the Korean quarantine was intended to prevent a deadly virus from spreading, and thus allows the film to use 'imagery of large groups of South Koreans walking through the streets wearing white surgical masks' (Barr, 2016). This imagery would have a marked affect on the film's Korean audience as 'South Korea, like many Asian countries, lived under the fear of the SARS virus outbreak in 2003' (Barr, 2016). Therefore, much like how the images of nuclear devastation in *Gojira* played on the fears of its contemporary Japanese audience, *The Host* uses the imagery of quarantines and white surgical masks to evoke the anxieties of its twenty-first century Korean audience. Another similarity between the two seminal Kaiju films, as well as Kaiju cinema in general, is their use of a nihilistic ending. Typical American monster films, such as the aforementioned *The Beast from 20,000 Fathoms* (1953), will usually end with the heroic scientists or government officials celebrating their triumph over the monster. This is not the case in Kaiju cinema. As mentioned before, *Gojira* ends with Professor Yamane pondering the effects of Godzilla's existence upon the world, and whether humanity's continued testing of nuclear weapons will result in the creation of more destructive monsters, negating a happy ending for one troubled with the grim possibilities of what the future may hold. Fifty-two years later, *The Host* would also use a nihilistic ending to great effect, as the film ends with the main character, Gang-du watching a Washington press conference on television in which the 'government officials are explaining away the recent Korean Virus Crisis as merely "misinformation"' (Grant, 2013).

106

Gang-du then turns off the television because 'as he says, nothing good is on' (Grant, 2013), perhaps suggesting that it is pointless to even engage with governmental proceedings, as nothing will change and no lessons have been learned from the Han River monster's attack.

(Picture copyright of Warner Bros.).

The Host continues the long standing tradition in Kaiju cinema of highlighting issues that were of great importance to its intended audience, which began with *Gojira* in 1954. Much the same as its genre ancestor, *The Host* was released to enormous success, becoming (at the time) the most profitable Korean made film ever, raking in over $89 million worldwide (Box Office Mojo, 2007), as well as becoming a critical darling, seen most evidently in the film's 93% approval rating on the film review website Rotten Tomatoes (Rotten Tomatoes, 2007). It also had a marked effect on the worldwide perception of the Kaiju genre, which was seen by most critics a 'camp phenomenon' (McCorkle and Rhoads, 2018) due to the process of Americanization that many Kaiju films went through in order to (in the eyes of American distributors) make the films more palatable for American audiences, which saw many of the films heavily edited and 'marred by illogical changes, additional scenes and poor translation' and would in turn lead to the global misunderstanding of the Kaiju genre. *The Host,* while not completely destroying this perception, certainly made great strides towards giving the Kaiju genre its deserved cultural reverence. This is seen most evidently in the recent upsurge of Hollywood produced Kaiju films in the decade since the film's release, clearly showing an increase in the public's appetite for Kaiju stories, with films such as *Cloverfield* (2008), *Pacific Rim* (2013) and *Kong: Skull Island* (2017) proving to be top earners at the box office. The greatest example of this change is Gareth Edwards' stellar 2014 remake of *Godzilla,* which followed the lead of both *Gojira* and *The Host* before it by becoming the first American produced Kaiju film to use its story and monsters to highlight the anxieties of its modern audience, in this case, feelings of unease in regards to environmental disaster. Thanks to *The Host,* which itself owes a great debt to *Gojira,* the future of Kaiju cinema and its custom of commenting on contemporary societal worries looks brighter than ever before, as fans the world over look forward to both the sequel to Edwards' remake in 2019 and Godzilla's long awaited rematch with King Kong the following year.

(**Nathan Waring** is a student from Belfast currently studying Film Studies at Manchester Met).

(Picture copyright of Hanna-Barbera Productions/Toho Company).

RETROSPECTIVE: DR. TERROR'S VAULT OF HORROR

by David Brilliance

(Picture copyright of the BBC).

The Horror Double Bill seasons that had thrilled kids and adults alike on BBC2 through the latter half of the 1970s/early 1980s, had been just a fond memory for horror fans for many years. But in the Autumn of 1993, the BBC resurrected the double bill format, with a series of films that not only had an on-screen host but a title sequence too! The first series featuring Dr. Terror must have been a success, as there was another series in late 1994, (but only one film per week in that one), and a third and final series appeared in 1996 (ditto). Grab a candle, a Halloween mask, and a book of horror film facts/clichés and we'll explore them further...

DR. TERROR'S VAULT OF HORROR, SERIES 1 (1993)

Friday Sept 10, 23.15.
Vamp (1986)
The Mask of Satan (1961)

After an intro sequence showing the good Dr. Terror looking at clips from *Curse of Frankenstein* and *Blood of Dracula* through some old-fashioned binoculars, the season kicked off with a crap 1980s comedy/horror starring Grace Jones, followed by a classic Italian film with the iconic Barbara Steele as a witch who gets a mask of spikes hammered into her face at the beginning. Rather stupidly, neither of these films appealed to me back then, so I didn't bother to watch them, let alone tape them! I've still got the bruises from where I've been kicking myself ever since.

Friday Sept 17, 23.25.
The Guardian (1990)
From Hell it Came (1957)

Whoever was behind selecting the films in this season must have been barking mad, to have considered trees as the subject for the second week's double bill! They can't have been that stumped for suitable subjects to cover at this point! Both films are poor, *The Guardian* generally considered another in the line of rotten films that William Friedkin followed up *The*

Exorcist with, and has Jenny Seagrove as a nanny who intends sacrificing children to a tree god, while *From Hell it Came* has Tod Andrews involved with a walking tree stump which contains the soul of a wrongly-executed man. Can you blame me for choosing to give these two a miss?

(Picture copyright of Galatea Film).

Friday Sept 24, 23.30.
The Curse of Frankenstein (1957)
Blood of Dracula (1957)

Ah, the first proper 'Hammer Horror' double bill, *The Curse of Frankenstein* is a landmark classic, made real stars of Peter Cushing and Christopher Lee, and put Hammer films (and Bray Studios) on the map. The only problem with this screening was the fact that the BBC, or ITV, screened the film every other year and a film that hadn't been shown to excess may have been preferable. *Blood of Dracula*, by contrast was a TV rarity. Not surprising really, as it is rubbish. Sandra Harrison plays a teenage girl who becomes a vampire after being hypnotised at a sinister girls' school. Nice make-up, pity about the film. I taped Curse...

Friday Oct 1, 23.05.

Horror Express (1972)
The Comedy of Terrors (1963)

Horror stars galore this week, with Cushing and Lee in *Horror Express*, sharing a train travelling through Siberia with a strange alien creature - no, not Telly Savalas! - which drains its victims' minds. A good, but overrated, film. *The Comedy of Terrors* toplines Boris Karloff, Vincent Price, Peter Lorre and Basil Rathbone (the latter two not really horror stars, but often fondly misremembered as such) in a humorous piece about undertakers creating their own business. I missed both these films back then, due to my being out conducting my charity work in the East End...

Friday Oct 8, 23.10.
Crucible of Terror (1971)
The Beast with Five Fingers (1946)

'Hands' were the subject on this week. In the first film, Mike Raven stars as a sculptor in Cornwall who has a sinister secret involving women and wax. Raven always wanted to be a bona fide horror star but, although he looks quite creepy, his lisping voice worked against him. The film overall is just okay. *The Beast with Five Fingers* has a disembodied hand scuttling about, playing the piano and generally causing chaos. It all turns out to be a figment of Peter Lorre's imagination, in a film notorious for it's silly ending. I videotaped both these films.

Friday Oct 15, 23.15.
Twins of Evil (1971)
Terror From the Year 5000 (1958)

After their success in week one, Dr. Terror brought back more evil women for week six. A shame the better of the two came first, as it meant there was really no incentive to sit through the second, which is a crappy B movie of the sort that seemed to appear a lot during this season - had the BBC acquired a job lot of them? *Twins of Evil* is a Hammer film, part of their Karnstein trilogy, and has Peter Cushing as the leader of a fanatical Brotherhood who are battling Count Karnstein. One of Cushing's sexy nieces has been vampirised by Karnstein, and so the gloves are off. This was followed by the rotten *Terror From the Year 5000*, a lame SF film which has Salome Jens as a female mutant from the future being brought back in time by scientist Ward Costello. This could have been good, in an *Outer Limits*-type way, but it has more in common with *Robot Monster* and *Plan 9 From Outer Space*. I taped *Twins of Evil* back then, but didn't bother with the other.

Friday Oct 22, 23.50.
Blood of the Vampire (1958)
I Don't Want to be Born (1975)

The theme for Week seven was either 'films which aren't quite classics but are very good anyway', or 'dwarves'. I'll leave it for you to decide. The first film has Donald Wolfitt as a character who is a cross between Dracula and Frankenstein, but not as good as either. The second has Joan Collins being cursed by a dwarf to give birth to a hideous, evil baby. Great flashback scene, complete with creepy score, and no dialogue until the dwarf suddenly appears, shouting and screaming at Collins. This made me jump when I first saw the film, back in the 1980s. I tried to tape it here, but the tape ran out and I lost the last fifteen minutes!

Friday Oct 29, 23.20.
The Gate (1987)
I Was a Teenage Frankenstein (1957).

The theme for this week was 'crap films'. It's hard to say which decade was the worst for decent horror films, the 1950s or the 1980s, but here we get examples of both. *The Gate* has a twelve year old boy discovering a gateway to Hell in his backyard, and being assaulted by moths, disembodied arms, and some quite cute little demons! The latter has Whit Bissell as a scientist who repairs teenager Gary Conway's injuries after a car crash, and makes him look pretty revolting in the

113

process. As with *Blood of Dracula*, good make-up wasted on a crummy film. I didn't bother with either of these two, as my charity work took precedence...

(Picture copyright of New Century Entertainment Corporation).

Friday Nov 5, 23.10.
The Haunted House of Horror (1969)
The House on Haunted Hill (1958)

Well, the theme for Week nine was clear, though it's a surprising fact that a horror film starring Frankie Avalon turns out be a lot better than one that headlines Vincent Price - *The Haunted House of Horror* is surprisingly entertaining, despite having no supernatural haunting involved. It's a sort of stalk n' slash film years before they became fashionable and provides a lot of interest watching the dated fashions, plus seeing lots of faces familiar to British TV viewers - there's George (*UFO*) Sewell and Nicholas (*Tomorrow People*) Young, and Richard (*Man About the House*) O'Sullivan. *The House on Haunted Hill* is a lot less interesting despite Price's presence, and it was all I could do to stay awake.

114

Friday Nov 12, 23.15.
The Lost Boys (1987)
I Was a Teenage Werewolf (1957).

This week was again devoted to 'crap films'. I've never been able to sit through *The Lost Boys*, a vampire film which makes the *Twilight* films look good! *I Was a Teenage Werewolf* has Michael Landon as a student who is hypnotised into becoming a werewolf. It's as good as it sounds - ie; not very! I avoided both of these back then - with more of my all-consuming charity work in the offing, it wasn't difficult.

Friday Nov 19, 23.40.
April Fools Day (1986)
Cat's Eye (1985)

Two agreeable 1980s horrors this week, the first a stalk n' slash, with twin sisters Buffy and Muffy. One is normal, the other a psycho who subjects guests at an island party to April Fools jokes which turn out to be quite real, and deadly! *Cat's Eye* is an anthology of three Stephen King stories, only one of which has a supernatural element. A very enjoyable film, all the same. Why I didn't tape these two is anyone's guess - maybe I'd ran out of blank videos?

(Picture copyright of Dino De Laurentiis Company).

Fri Nov 26.

The theme for this week was Children In Need, as Dr Terror took a week off.

Fri Dec 3, 23.05.
Countess Dracula (1971)
Voodoo Woman (1957)

Those 'evil women' get everywhere! Here's more, in two films of varying quality - I'm wasn't really impressed with *Countess Dracula*, the weakest of the four horrors the overrated Ingrid Pitt appeared in, in the early '70s. It has a naff, documentary-style look to it (the equally tedious *Demons of the Mind*, made by Hammer, has the same sort of look), and is just average. *Voodoo Woman* is terrible, with Tom Conway as a scientist who uses voodoo and hypnotism to create a female monster in the jungle. I taped *Countess Dracula*, but didn't bother with the other.

Fri Dec 17, 00.10.
Hands of the Ripper (1971).

The season concluded with an excellent Hammer film, involving Anna Ripper, Jack's daughter, who commits a series of grisly murders whenever she is kissed in front of a flickering light. Good cast, good film, good season.

DR. TERROR'S VAULT OF HORROR, SERIES 2 (1994)

Fri Sept 9, 23.00.
The Fog (1980)

This second season had a rather childish, but likeable, intro, showing the good doctor at an amusement park, travelling around on a ghost train. Once that's over, he introduces the week's film, in this case a late 70s John Carpenter film, about

116

the ghosts of embittered sailors returning, in a creepy fog, to get revenge on the inhabitants of the coastal town where they were shipwrecked centuries ago. I'd seen this previously on the Beeb, but due to my charity work again, I didn't bother with it on this occasion.

Fri Sept 16, 23.00.
The Ghoul (1975)

The fact we get a glimpse of Veronica Carlson's stocking tops means that this dreary film has been overrated to a degree it doesn't deserve. It's not terrible, but it's not great either. Peter Cushing plays a man who lives in an isolated mansion at Land's End, with servants including an unhinged John Hurt, and his deformed mutant son (the 'ghoul' of the title), who he keeps locked in the attic and feeds on human blood. I'd seen it before, but didn't bother with it this time around. This was one of the very few films made by Tyburn, and Kevin Francis (Tyburn's head) is apparently blocking the release of them on disc. As far as I'm concerned, he can keep this one!

(Picture copyright of Tyburn Film Prosuctions Ltd.).

Fri Sept 23, 23.05.
The Unnamable Returns (1992)

This was a sequel to a 1988 film based on a story by H.P. Lovecraft, and it concerns a demon getting loose, and trying to mate with a young woman. The fact that David Warner is in the cast is its only real recommendation, and it is a typically rubbishy 90s horror. I didn't bother with this, as charity work intervened.

Fri Sept 30, 23.00.
Taste the Blood of Dracula (1970)

Suffice to say, this is a classic, very enjoyable and with some great characters. As Dr. Terror cheerily informed us in his intro, this was the fully uncut version, with all those scenes of murder by shovel etc intact, and with some brothel nudity. Something about the film was vaguely familiar, but I can't think what..

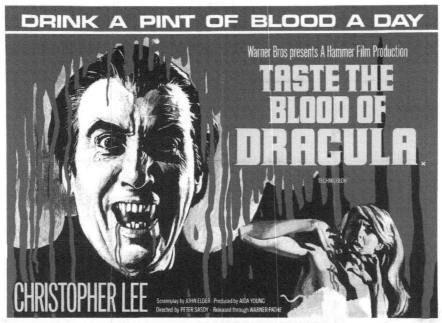

(Picture copyright of Hammer Films).

Fri Oct 7, 00.05.
A Study in Terror (1965)

This isn't a classic, but it's certainly a very enjoyable film. John Neville makes an adequate Sherlock Holmes, tracking down Jack the Ripper. It's more detective thriller than horror movie, but has a couple of nice creepy scenes. I remember my cousin always going on in the 70s, about this film he'd seen on a Friday night, where you see a woman walking around a street corner and suddenly a hand holding a knife appears...then it is revealed to be a butcher cutting up a pig! Turns out it was this. Once again, my charity work meant I had no money to spend on videotapes, so I couldn't record it.

Fri Oct 14, 23.45.
Legend of the Werewolf (1974)

Far better than *The Ghoul*, this is set in nineteenth century Paris, and has nice performances from Peter Cushing and Ron Moody. The werewolf make-up is similar to that in Hammer's *Curse of the Werewolf*, only not as good, and the film is quite unintentionally funny, which adds to it's entertainment factor. This is one film that Kevin Francis can release, and the sooner the better. If only to see the hilarious 'dog with human intelligence' again!

Fri Oct 21.
Golf was the theme for this week, so no Dr. Terror.

Fri Oct 28, 23.20.
Body Parts (1991)

Jeff Fahey stars in this one, as a prison psychologist who loses his arm in a car accident, and gets the arm of a serial killer grafted on in its place. It turns out to be a bit more complex than the average Hands of Orlac-type plot, but it's not really a very good film. I'd stopped my charity work for a bit, after my two friends and I had a very strange night...

Fri Nov 4, 00.25.
Curse of the Crimson Altar (1968)

I've always loved this one - Boris Karloff, Christopher Lee, Michael Gough, Barbara Steele (if you must, though personally, I'm no fan of hers), and that bloke from *Coronation Street*! Based on another Lovecraft tale, the horror content is slight but it's a very nice and cosy sort of film, with some memorable lines - I've often said 'good stuff' after drinking a glass of wine in someone's house! I recorded this one.

Fri Nov 11, 23.40.
The Mummy (1959)

On a par with *The Curse of Frankenstein*, and miles better than the boring *Dracula*, this 1959 Hammer film was receiving it's umpteenth UK TV screening here. Good to see it nonetheless, complete with Dr. Terror's intro, who waffles on about how the victims in *Mummy* movies have to get trapped in a corner and wait patiently for the Mummy to slowly limp up and strangle them! I didn't tape this, but only because I'd ran out of tape.

(Picture copyright of Hammer Films).

Fri Nov 18, 23.30.
The Legacy (1979)

An enjoyable British horror, with a group of people in a creepy old country house dying in various imaginative ways - the swimming pool sequence is a stand-out, but my favourite death in the film comes when Roger Daltrey (of The Who) gets a chicken bone stuck in his throat - even though he wasn't eating chicken at the time! The film has been described as 'ho-hum', but I like it.

Fri Dec 2 (the previous week missed due to Children In Need), 00.30.
Dr. Terror's House of Horrors (1964)

This is the first of the Amicus anthology series, a good film, with Chris Lee being made a monkey of by Michael Gough, then being troubled by 'wandering hand syndrome', this segment a stand-out. I videotaped this one, to replace the grainy version I had previously.

Fri Dec 9, 23.35.
Alligator (1980)

This is a good one, with an alligator in the sewers growing to huge size, and emerging to cause chaos. Henry Silva plays a hunter who ends up being eaten, and although the killer alligator ends up being blown to bits, there's a nice twist at the ending. I taped this too, and made it snappy!

(Picture copyright of Alligator Inc.).

Fri Dec 16, 00.20.
The Serpent and the Rainbow (1986)

The season ended with this fairly average Wes Craven shocker, involving voodoo and drugs. Michael Gough is in it, and the film involves a pharmaceutical company wanting to get hold of a drug that will act as a super anaesthetic, and turn people into zombies! Some gruesome stuff in this one, including a scorpion in someone's throat, and the hero being buried alive with a tarantula to keep him company! There's a happy ending anyway, but not for viewers because this was the last of this season.

DR. TERROR PRESENTS (1996)

Fri Sept 27, 23.55.
The House of Seven Corpses (1973)

After a gap, the third and final season appeared, this time with a naff game show-inspired intro each week. Most of the films in this shorter run weren't up to much either. This one involves a director making a film in a house that's genuinely haunted. He decides to have the cast act out the deaths of those who were killed in the place for real - bad idea, as it summons a creepy ghoul that starts to kill everyone. Faith Domergue and John Carradine are in it, but it's just average overall, and I didn't tape it.

Fri Oct 4, 00.05.
The Asphyx (1972)

I haven't seen this for many years, but I remember it as being okay. Robert Stephens and Robert Powell star as two Victorian scientists who try to capture the 'Asphyx', which is a force which comes and collects souls of those who are about to die. There's a guillotining scene, but that's all I can recall. One to watch for on DVD/Blu-Ray, I think.

Fri Oct 11, 00.40.
Devils of Darkness (1964)

This is a very boring and un-atmospheric film, set in France, and involving vampires who practice human sacrifice. It has the same sort of colourful, Hollywood musical look to it that certain Hammer films from the late 1950s/early 1960s had, which is no good for what is supposed to be a creepy horror film. Eminently missable - and I did.

Fri Oct 18, 00.40.
The Beast in the Cellar (1971)

Not a classic, but another enjoyable film from Tigon, with Beryl Reid and Flora Robson as sisters who walled their brother up alive in the cellar so he wouldn't be called up for national service! He ends up looking a bit like the beggar in Hammer's _Curse of the Werewolf_, but is only properly seen at the end. Some gory bits including a surprising scene where Reid pushes a corpse's dislodged eye back in, after her brother had torn it out! I taped this one.

(Picture copyright of Tigon British Film Productions).

Fri Oct 25, 00.50.
A Child For Satan (1991)

This is a TV movie, but the golden age of great horror TV movies had long since passed, and so this is a bit rubbish. It involves two virginal births, one for the Devil, one for God, and a priest gets bothered by some Satanists who are out to stop him killing the Devil's child. I didn't watch all of this back then, as it was so riveting I fell asleep!

Fri Nov 1, 00.05.
Ghost Story (1981)

You'd think that the presence of people like Fred Astaire and Douglas Fairbanks Jnr. in a horror film would be enough to sink it, but this isn't all that bad. It's about a group of four old men who regale each other with scary stories, and end up being haunted by a young woman who brings about their deaths for some past crime. I didn't even know this was on all those years ago, which shows how much of an impression this lacklustre season made on me!

Fri Nov 8, 00.35.
Dr. Giggles (1992)

This involves a mad doctor, nicknamed 'Giggles' because of his spine-chilling laugh, who escapes from a asylum, and goes on a killing spree. Not up to much, but a nice black comedy ending. I gave this a miss.

(Picture copyright of Dark Horse Entertainment).

Fri Nov 15, 00.20.

Phantasm (1979)

The last offering from the good doctor is a cult film, about a sinister mortician, nicknamed 'The Tall Man', who raises the dead as his dwarf henchmen. Mike Baldwin (no relation to the one in *Coronation Street*, sadly - now that would have been really entertaining!) is the kid who rumbles him. This was a very successful film, and led to several sequels, but I still haven't seen any of them!

(Picture copyright of New Breed Productions Inc.).

PETER CUSHING: A TRIBUTE

by Owen Quinn

Ask anyone to name an actor associated with British horror and two will always come up - Peter Cushing and Christopher Lee.

I sadly never got to meet Peter Cushing, which I regret. He terrified me in the Hammer horror movies and swept me along in his battles with the Daleks.

It is nearly twenty five years since Peter died and yet it seems he is still around. I think it is fair to say that although he is not the first actor to be brought back via CGI, he is the first to be so at the forefront of a story to the point kids couldn't tell that he wasn't real.

That moment in *Rogue One* when Grand Moff Tarkin turned to the camera and we saw Peter Cushing's face has divided many. Whether it is a good thing or not is a matter for another time but it did introduce one of our greatest actors to a whole new generation of children. Cushing in the first *Star Wars* movie brought a grandeur to the proceedings that contributed immensely to the movie's success. He did admit that that he wondered what a Grand Moff was and initially thought it was a moth. He also said he hadn't a clue what was going on as it was for children and he took roles that he thought people would like to see him in. Despite this lack of understanding, his cold, emotionless slaughter of an entire planet enthralled audiences. He was the true villain of the piece and when you look at it Darth Vader was his lackey, even if Tarkin ruled the galaxy in comfy slippers. Guy Henry did a great job in capturing Cushing's take on Tarkin, a man focused entirely on dominating the galaxy with his super weapon.

Did you know that somewhere in the world at any given time, a Peter Cushing movie is being shown? Known throughout the industry as a consummate gentleman, Peter was also an active writer whose career spanned six decades. He has played virtually everything from Van Helsing to Sherlock Holmes to Doctor Who himself and endures to this day in every performance. He was also asked to play the Doctor on television but declined. His reasons were simple: it wasn't his cup of tea and he didn't like the Daleks!

There are few actors who can span generations but Peter

was one of them. His distinctive timeless features adorned many a screen big and small in over one hundred movies and shows like *Space 1999*. His rich voice enhanced many a radio play. He was adored by everyone, young and old alike. Children loved him as the Doctor because he portrayed him as a kindly old grandfather with a hint of mischief in his eye, while adults loved him staking Dracula, spearing mummies or battling the Seven Golden Vampires. Even his lesser roles – such as in *Night of the Big Heat*, where he simply played an islander who loved a pint in his local – were thoughtfully played by the actor. One thing you could never do was forget Peter Cushing and fans just lit up whenever and wherever he appeared.

(Picture copyright of Hammer Films).

His career began in the British theatre before making a name for himself in Hollywood in movies like *The Man in the Iron Mask* and *A Chump in Oxford*. Returning to his homeland during the Second World War, he began working in television in shows like *1984*. But the British film industry was booming and a company called Hammer began making horror movies which would define the careers of Peter and Christopher Lee alike.

To the world they are the British horror industry and no matter how naff the script was – and there were some naff ones – it was the sincere and straight way the actors played the roles that managed to lift them beyond mediocrity. Famously, whilst playing Sherlock Holmes, Peter didn't like the taste of a pipe and kept a glass of milk on hand to take away the taste. Again don't forget the slippers in *Star Wars*.

Despite his stardom and international success, Peter feared typecasting like many actors, so to take this away he took on the role of Doctor Who in two movies for Amicus, Hammer's main rivals. He played him as a grandfather, fiercely protective of his granddaughters, who had invented a time machine, the Tardis, in his back garden. Both movies had Peter face off against the Daleks in glorious technicolour. It was these movies that inspired today's new generation of Daleks for Matt Smith. It speaks volumes about Peter's character that he wasn't even aware how loved he was and, as I said, he could walk across any medium and immediately be loved by fans.

(Picture copyright of AARU Productions/British Lion Films).

No matter where he appeared, his presence lit up the room and gave a gravitas to any scene, as seen in *Space 1999* where he played Raan and also as the only high profile actor who has appeared in both the old and new *Avengers* opposite Patrick McNee and featuring the Cybernauts.

129

Indeed, he was a favourite on *The Morecambe and Wise Show* where he endured the running joke of never getting paid for his services and eternally seeking that elusive fiver. This he would finally get on *This is Your Life* when Ernie appeared, Eric having passed on at this stage, and gave him that fiver before stealing it off him again. But that was Peter, loved by everyone, a perfectionist actor and a real star. Many so called celebrities of today who quite simply aren't famous for their talent could learn a lesson in star quality from Peter and indeed from his great friend Christopher Lee also. There was no tantrums or diva behaviour, just grounded acting which endeared them greatly to the crews they worked with.

He was married to his beloved Helen for many years before she died. And such was his humility he wrote to *Jim'll Fix It* to ask if he could have a rose named after his late wife. Who else among the so called stars of today would even think about doing that? They would simply fire a few thousand in someone's direction and make it happen. For Peter he had lost his soul mate in her passing and in an interview he said that her loss had left him where his only ambition was to join her one day. Life was all about killing time for him after this. One of my most prized possessions is a letter to me from Peter when I wrote to him back in the nineties asking for his autograph. He sent me the most beautiful letter about himself and thanked me for remarking on the fact that his wife had a rose named after her. It has to be the most touching letter from a celebrity I have ever received and as much as I loved the man then, in that moment, he was a hero. Not for the trappings of celebrity but for being a man whose loss became our loss and to acknowledge that in a letter was simply mind-blowing. That quality should be shown to all these newbie celebs. And every time I see him in a movie that letter springs to mind.

Not a religious man but one of strong ethical beliefs, Peter lived his life to the full as a poem left by Helen urged him to live it to the max but his grief had obvious physical effects on him. And that is why Peter is so loved to this day. When he hurt, the world hurt with him. He was the people's actor, no airs or graces and a gentleman to the end. He was quality, he was class, he was indomitable and he will never ever be forgotten.

I think we'll leave the last word to co star Christopher Lee. On Peter's death he said: "At some point in your lives, every one of you will notice that you have in your life one person, one friend whom you love and care for very much. That person is so close to you that you are able to share some things only with him. For example, you can call that friend and from the very first maniacal laugh or some other joke, you will know who is at the other end of that line. We used to do that so often. And then when that person is gone, there will be nothing like that in your life ever again."

There will never be his like again.

(Picture copyright of Lucasfilm/Twentieth Century Fox).

PHANTASMAGORIA REVIEWS

LITERATURE

RICOCHET by Tim Dry

You might think that the strange, exotic and, yes, erotic literary landscapes invoked by the likes of William Burroughs, Alan Ginsberg and Hunter S. Thompson were a phenomena of the 1950s and '60s. How wrong you would be. There are still writers out there whose talents lies with the words, the way they are formed, the way they are patterned, rather than the story they portray. One such is Tim Dry.

Some may know him as an actor in *Star Wars: Return of the Jedi* or as a performance artist, but as a writer he has yet again redefined himself.

This novella is the first volume in what will be a series of books based in the same chaosium. It is a place where words are your guide but will often betray your expectations. There is structure to it but not in the traditional sense and this is why comparison to the literary works of Burroughs and the poetry of Ginsberg is so apt.

For those wanting more from their reading than a simple plot or closely defined - perhaps the word should be caged - comedy, horror, or thrills, this is for you, though treat it gently as it can and will bite when you are least expecting it.

Ricochet is available to purchase from Amazon, Barnes & Noble, Books-A-Million, Bokus and Sears.

John Gilbert.

(Editor's note: This review first appeared in FEAR Magazine).

THE QLIPHOTH by Paul A. Green

Where do I begin? There is no way I can do complete justice to such a cleverly written book. But I will try to breakdown this twisty, turny, helter-skelter of awesomeness. Firstly I should say that I had to look up what a Qliphoth was/is. I found out it is part of the Jewish Kabbalah and means 'shell', 'husk' or 'peels'. It is seen as a representation of evil and impure spiritual forces.

So, to the story...

Set in the 1980s it centres around Lucas, a product of two extremely dysfunctional parents - Pauline, his mother (or smother), an overbearing, orderly women who is a teacher, and Nick, his hippie father, who is stuck in a mental hospital after using himself as a channel for occult practice. Talk about chalk and cheese. Lucas has dropped out of education and consequently life. The story starts when he finds himself on holiday with his mother, in the family holiday home in the West Country. Lucas is watching VHS tapes that he has found in his mum's room. He is looking for a memory he has of his parents being on a TV show in the hope that it will explain what happened to his dad. What he finds is a documentary about mental illness with his father as the main protagonist.

Then his mum walks in and after an almighty row, Lucas decides he's going to find his father, who coincidentally is in the local mental institution several miles away.

Lucas storms out and Pauline is powerless to stop him. On his way to said mental hospital, Lucas finds himself at the local railway station - Western Grand Junction Station, which on first appearance seems to be abandoned. Then he meets Controller Buttivant and strikes up a rather odd conversation. He is subsequently coerced into accepting a lift from a rather large European man, Mr Kraskolkyn. Lucas is really up the junction now as he seems to have passed into another reality where he meets some very eccentric characters.

Meanwhile, back in the 'real' world, Pauline has reported her son missing and goes in search of a man named Larry. Larry is sort of where the problem started. You see, back in the 1960s, Nick (Pauline's ex-husband) owned a shop called The Great British Time Machine. Larry sold him some books and papers, that turned out to be of the occult Crowelian variety. She believes Larry has the answers to Nick's insanity and where her son may have gone. All this while balancing a teaching job in a high school where something is not quite kosher.

Nick has troubles of his own. He has teamed up with a fellow inmate from the asylum - Wolfbane. He thinks Wolfbane can help him escape and get back to his son Lucas, whom he knows is in trouble because of his occult abilities. Wolfbane won't leave without Tanya, another inmate, so Nick agrees and the three of them break out. Nick believes that Wolfbane is there to help him but Wolfbane has his own agenda. An agenda that becomes apparent when they meet up with a certain Mr Kraskolkyn.

The story moves between the three main characters, Lucas and his parents, Pauline and Nick, and with each character we get a snippet of what's going on in their world and how it unknowingly touches the others. There is so much more to this book than what I have written though. It is full of diverse and wonderfully written characters, all woven together to produce a story that is unlike any other. Paul Green's writing reminds me of Douglas Adams' - it is bizarre and quirky in the the most delicious way. He writes with a real knowledge of his subject matter too. I personally felt the chapters about Pauline and her teaching experiences were perhaps semi-auto-biographical, as Paul Green himself was a teacher, which thank goodness he gave up to write.

A great read and one that I would highly recommend.

The Qliphoth is available to purchase from Amazon.

Helen Scott.

LOUISVILLE'S STRANGE AND UNUSUAL HAUNTS by Jacob & Jenny Floyd

This is the third of Jacob's books I have reviewed. The first was *The Pleasure Hunt*, his debut novel (in issue 3), and then *Kentucky's Haunted Mansions* (issue 4), written with his wife Jenny, as is this one. I have sort of worked backwards, because I think this is actually their first book.

Unlike *Kentucky's Haunted Mansions*, which focuses on haunted houses, this book has a range of haunts. Just as the title suggests some are strange and all are unusual. It is a bit of this and and a bit of that. What do I mean? Well, no two accounts are the same and Jenny and Jacob delight in the telling of a ghostly tale. There is no pretence, in that if they can't explain it or have been unable to get any evidence then they tell you that. You, the reader get to make up your own mind and I like that. Accounts are divided into locations ranging from graveyards and cemeteries, as you'd expect, to shops, restaurants, bars and haunted lodgings.

I was fascinated by the account of a cafe where no one was able to sustain a business there. Despite remodelling it, the businesses would always flop, until Cafe 360 moved in. A waitress gives an account to the 'Frightening Floyds' of the second floor being haunted. This includes hearing footsteps running, lights going on and off and voices being heard. The waitress recounts how when the current owners went to remodel the second floor 'something' made them stop. Whatever it was, it looks like they did the right thing because their business has succeeded where multiple others have failed. I think the spirit likes things just how they are.

There is another account of Jenny recording a voice saying 'words such as penny, coins, cards' at the grave of a magician called Harry Collins. The grave is in Cave Hill cemetery, where quite a few famous people are buried, including Col Harland Sanders and Muhammad Ali. Jenny and Jacob had visited the cemetery on several occasions because they had heard accounts of floating orbs, disembodied voices and tombstones falling over as if they'd been pushed. They wanted to investigate these multiple claims of sightings. What they actually recorded on their spirit box proved to them that paranormal activity was evident in the cemetery.

As with *Kentucky's Haunted Mansions*, this book does not try to convince you to believe. What it does is leave bread crumbs for you to follow and accounts for you to ruminate and debate over. You don't have to be a believer to enjoy this book. In fact I think if you are a sceptic then it will challenge your views and lead to the debate that I mentioned earlier. I liked how it was factual but not impersonal and not forceful in its views of the accounts recorded. I feel I also have to mention Jenny's photographs as for me they added to the ambience of the book.

Jenny and Jacob Floyd have done it again...I want to believe.

Louisville's Strange and Unusual Haunts is available to purchase from Amazon.

Helen Scott.

THEM by James Watts

Ray Sanders is a young man who has to make a return to his home town of Maple Grove, Alabama, for the funeral of his beloved mother. She died suddenly in what is believed to be natural causes, but in reality was rather unnatural and unpleasant circumstances. After her funeral, Ray decides to hang around town for a while, catching up with some old friends, like his close cousin, Roy, and his ex-girlfriend, Beth. But he is soon plagued by intense nightmares and something quite nasty appears to be residing in his basement cellar. When people from Maple Grove begin turning up dead in mysterious ways, Ray realises he must confront an old family secret head-on, which is also connected to the town's origins and some creatures not of this world.

As I was reading this work, I was instantly struck by how author Watts' main strength is in his imagined characters and how he builds his story around them, similar to what Stephen King does in his books. This is very much the tale of the lives and loves of said characters, Ray being the backbone of the events depicted. The horror and bad things that happen to them come secondary to these fully-formed fictional people brought to life on the pages. Watts' knows his creations well and allows the reader to care for their collective plight with ease. Even the secondary characters, like the drug dealer and his stoner sidekick, are very well formed and believable.

The author also retains a sense of mystery throughout, with the true nature and intentions of the monsters (both human and non-human) gradually revealed as the plot proceeds. I found myself wanting to know more about why these creatures were possessing the bodies of local animals and then bumping off the human populace, but Watts keeps his cards close to his chest, in turn keeping the reader longing for more, all the while creating dramatic tension more and more.

I do love a good villain and the human bad guy at the centre of the unfolding events, Judd Atkins, is very well written also, his greed and selfishness totally believable due to the writer's skill of depiction of him. He was probably my favourite character.

I urge you to give this book a go and look forward to hearing about what James Watts has in store next. Recommended.

Them is available to purchase from Amazon, Barnes & Noble, Books-A-Million, Chapters, Powell's, Waterstones, Foyles and Northshire.

Trevor Kennedy.

FILM

HEREDITARY (2018)

(Picture copyright of PalmStar Media).

Directed by Ari Aster.

Written by Ari Aster.

Starring Toni Collette, Milly Shapiro, Gabriel Byrne, Alex Wolff and more.

(N.B. To me, creepy kids in horror films are just another boring cliche, now done to death, which is why I was somewhat apprehensive going into the cinema to view this film, going by what I saw in the trailer. I need not have worried though, as the trailer is misleading and the creepy kid in question plays just a part of a much bigger overall plot.)

As a contemporary American family mourns the loss of their maternal grandmother/mother figure, a series of odd occurrences soon leads them to further tragedy and the unravelling of dark disclosures of an occult nature involving a demonic King of Hell named Paimon.

Let's not mess around here, this film is breathtakingly

fantastic. In the last issue of this publication, I boldly stated that *Ghost Stories* was the best new horror release in years, but it now very much has a rival in those stakes with director/writer Ari Aster's debut feature. It may be unfair to compare the two, however, as they are both very different films, in that while *Ghost Stories* is great fun with scares aplenty in a tongue-in-cheek sort of way, *Hereditary* is played out in the most serious of manners, and I don't think it would work any other way. Adult horror, if you will.

This newly released American movie is very much in the style of old school horror, in the sense that it is subtle and builds the tension and drama as the plot unfolds gradually. It does not rely on jump scares either, like most modern horror film rubbish like *The Conjuring* series does.

It is deeply unsettling, genuinely creepy and shocking in parts, with a startling finale, and overall it reminded me in parts of horror cinema classics like *Rosemary's Baby* and *Don't Look Now*. This work of art is now one of the very few pieces of fiction to actually scare me and remain in my thoughts long after. That ending really got under my skin and I am speaking as someone who considers himself highly desensitised after a lifetime of the watching and reading of hardcore horror. A full twenty-four hours after watching it (and at time of writing), I still can't shake its power and imagery from my mind.

I think we may even be entering a golden age of horror and I'm not just saying this because of my own creative interests in the field. Fans have had enough of the rubbish Hollywood has been pumping out for years in recent times, i.e. tiresome remakes and sequels and PG-13 rated dross like the aforementioned *The Conjuring* and *Insidious*. We now seem to be getting back to basics with genuine, original (with a nudge and wink to the classics of the 1970s etc) films like this and *Ghost Stories* in the space of just a couple of months of each other.

It is also worth noting that the acting on display here is of an extremely high standard, especially from Australian actress Toni Collette as the disturbed mother.

This is an absolutely fantastic film which disturbed and unsettling me immensely (in that great horror film way!). I look forward to hearing and seeing more from Ari Aster in the future. Brilliant!

Trevor Kennedy.

(Picture copyright of PalmStar Media).

AVENGERS: INFINITY WAR (2018)

Directed by Anthony Russo and Joe Russo.

Written by Christopher Markus (screenplay by), Stephen McFeely (screenplay by), Stan Lee and more.

Starring Robert Downey Jr., Chris Hemsworth, Mark Ruffalo, Scarlett Johansson and more.

I am sure I have announced this a trillion times previously but it is very hard to get a sole hardcore DC fan (such as me) to watch a Marvel movie let alone review one! So give me credit first and foremost for scribing some thoughts and concepts here, haha.

A trivial fact that persuaded me to actually go and see this sequel is that I am a die-hard Goonies fan. And back in the day, *The Goonies* starred a lad called Josh Brolin, who has now leapt to big bad things as the mad titan Thanos in this Hollywood phenomenon. Seems a far-fetched connection right?

(Picture copyright of Marvel Studios).

Avengers: Infinity War brings together a plethora of heroes and villains which have featured across all eighteen instalments of the Marvel Universe and it comprises a solid list of contenders including Chris Evans, Robert Downey Jr., Scarlett Johansson, Chris Hemsworth, Mark Ruffalo and much more.

The plot goes something like this – An unhinged Thanos uses his children to hunt down six Infinity stones which will send half of the human race to the brink of destruction. His mission is to break Vision by retrieving the Mind Stone since

144

he already acquired the blue Space Stone Loki pocketed before the end of *Thor: Ragnarok*.

Whilst this is happening at the forefront of the film, our heroes Tony Stark and Bruce Banner meet up with Dr Strange and Wong and before you know it, Peter Parker aka Spider-man joins the good side to go up against the purple baddie.

Meanwhile, Thanos' children, Maw and Obsidian, arrive in New York to seize the Time Stone from Strange and so Stark, Strange, Wong and Peter Parker set to confront them as Banner is unable to transform into the Hulk, having been traumatized by his defeat at the hands of Thanos. In the process, Strange is incapacitated and captured and though you may think Banner is useless in this, he does in fact contact the rest of the Avengers to warn them, thank goodness!

In Scotland, Vision and Wanda Maximoff are ambushed by Thanos' other children, Midnight and Gaive, and it's only then that Vision suggests that Maximoff should destroy the Mind Stone in his forehead to prevent Thanos from retrieving it. However, easier said than done when the only real way of extracting it would signify a trip to Wakanda. Also, we cannot forget about our space friends from the *Guardians of the Galaxy* who happen to befriend Thor – to clarify, that's the usual posse of Star-Lord, Groot, Rocket, Drax, Gamora and Mantis who warn Thor of Thanos' twisted will on reality.

Thor realises Thanos will go after the Reality Stone which is in the possession of the Collector in Knowhere, so whilst he heads on to retrieve a weapon called Stormbreaker from the dwarven planet Nidavellir, Gamora, Drax and Mantis accompany each other to Knowhere where Thanos ambushes them and does indeed nab the Reality Stone. At the same time, he takes Gamora back with him, already mind reading from her the whereabouts of the Soul Stone. So the pair travel to the planet of the Soul Stone and Thanos learns from Red Skull (the stone's keeper) that the only way he can possess this stone is if he sacrifices someone he truly loves. And that is the unfortunate end of Gamora.

Remember earlier I said Dr Strange was kidnapped? Well, Stark and Parker rescue him from Maw's wrath and then head on to Titan to meet up with Drax, Mantis and Quill and make plans to fight against Thanos. Managing to engage him and subdue him, Stark and Parker snatch Thano's Infinity gauntlet away whilst Mantis calms Thanos down. However Quill has deduced that Gamora has been killed by Thanos by this stage and reacts towards him, breaking the group's grip on Thanos. This then allows Dr Strange to surrender the Time Stone in order to save Stark and see Thanos depart Titan to get the next stone – the Mind Stone.

Despite our team heading to Wakanda to allow Shuri to attempt to extract the Mind Stone from Vision, Thanos' outsider army begin attacking the zone – alas Shuri is unsuccessful and a tearful Maximoff destroys the still implanted stone in Vision's head which backfires and instead, Thanos reverses the event with the Time Stone to pry the Mind Stone from Vision, killing him as a consequence.

(Picture copyright of Marvel Studios).

It's Thor to the rescue with Stormbreaker which he pushes through Thanos' chest however the purple beast continues to survive and teleports away with the gauntlet, achieving his goal.

This is when the viewer sadly realises that more than half the cast are being wiped out as Groot, Parker, Quill, Strange, T'Challa, Wilson, Drax, Mantis and Maximoff all dissolve into ash. Same goes for Rogers, Rocket, Thor and Banner amongst a few others who remain heroes. On Titan, only Nebula and Stark are left alive.

And then at the very end of the film, S.H.I.E.L.D agents are left to witness the half destruction of humanity before they themselves crumple into nothing but ultimately, Director Nick Fury sends an SOS to Captain Marvel...

The ending sets up the next one beautifully because there is clearly another one in the pipeline for next year. C'mon it's Marvel! Of course there is. They don't waste much time, however I must say for an extremely biased DC fan like myself, this film earned its merits!

Allison Weir.

DEADPOOL 2 (2018)

Directed by David Leitch.

Written by Rhett Reese, Paul Wernick and Ryan Reynolds.

Starring Ryan Reynolds, Morena Baccarin, Josh Brolin, Zazzie Beets, Brianna Hildebrand, Julian Dennison and more.

I am a sucker for an anti-hero, from the Watchmen and Judge Dredd, to Batman and the Punisher. Deadpool is another one whom I now have a soft spot for. I think this is because he wasn't born a mutant, like the X-Men, but instead, like Peter Parker and the Fantastic Four, had mutation thrust upon him. Life dealt him a cruel blow - cancer - it literally could happen to any of us. Mr Pool (as Dopinder the cabbie calls him) is just trying to make lemonade out of all the lemons life's given him.

The hilarious Bondesque title sequence at the beginning is a sign that this is just pure escapism and entertainment. And as sequels go this isn't bad at all, in fact I've seen it twice. What they have done is crafted a storyline that opens up a whole franchise potential, which always makes me apprehensive because of the potential of over saturation, Avengers being a case in point.

In this sequel we see Wade Wilson aka Mr Pool, living life with his bae Vanessa (Morena Baccairn), talking about having kids and doing the whole family thing. That is until Vanessa is killed when Wade is attacked at home. Life is over as he knows it. So Deadpool being Deadpool tries to end it all, because without Vanessa, what's the point? That is until he is recruited by Colossus (Stefan Kapicic) and Negasonic (Brianna Hildebrand) as a trainee X-Man.

(Picture copyright of Marvel Entertainment).

Whilst out on his first X-Men call to an orphanage, he meets

Russell aka Firefist (Julian Dennison) a tortured boy intent on killing his tortures, the orphanage staff. Never being one to follow the rules, or in this case Colossus' instructions, Deadpool sets about taking the boy's side and all havoc lets loose. The upshot is that Deadpool and Firefist find themselves sharing a cell in maximum security. That is until Cable (Josh Brolin), a genetically enhanced soldier from the future, shows up to kill Russell.

Russell, you see, grows up to be a very bad man and kills Cable's family. So Cable has travelled back in time to kill him before he can kill them. Meanwhile, Wade is having visions of Vanessa who is telling him to essentially save the kid. Russell is his raison d'etre. This means Cable is his enemy and it gets worse because the kid's only gone and teamed up with Juggernaut. Deadpool sets about building his own team to go get Russell. That in itself is comedy gold but it gets better...bring on the excellent soundtrack, tongue in cheek jokes and pew, pew, pew.

I won't tell you the end, but I will say this - the role of Deadpool was made for Reynolds, it fits him well. The supporting cast are also a huge part of what makes this film work. Eddie Marsan (*Ray Donovan, The World's End, Filth*) is great as the evil head of the orphanage. Karan Soni reprises his role as Dopinder and Leslie Uggams is back as Blind Al. It also introduces some new characters, Domino (Zazzie Beets) and Yukio (Shiori Katsuna), who I'm sure we'll see more of. Go see it for yourselves.

Helen Scott.

SOLO: A STAR WARS STORY (2018)

Directed by Ron Howard.

Written by Jonathan Kasdan, Lawrence Kasdan and George Lucas (characters).

Starring Alden Ehrenreich, Woody Harrelson, Emilia Clarke and more.

Take your mind back to the year of 1999. After sixteen years, a new *Star Wars* movie was coming out. What's more, it was reported that the film was going to explore the world before the original trilogy. Fans were losing what minds that they possessed in the first place.

In came an apple cheeked, wide-eyed, innocent little boy. This little boy was a dedicated *Star Wars* fan. Upon learning that this new movie was coming out, the little boy did what he could to ensure that he would go see it: he collected all the pennies he could find, snatched away any change that was left unattended, and even stood on a busy street corner with a cardboard sign around his neck that read, "You can spit on me for $.25". Then, once enough money had been collected for a ticket, the little boy went to see that new *Star Wars* movie.

That is when the little boy learned what betrayal was, for that movie was *Star Wars Episode 1: The Phantom Menace*. And, for a further twist, I can reveal that little boy was me.

So, going in to see *Solo: A Star Wars Story*, you can rest assured that I have a weaponized skepticism in regards to *Star Wars* prequels.

This movie follows the well-known and titular character, Han Solo (Alden Ehrenreich) on his journey to become the person that audiences know from the original trilogy. Along the way he is joined by the tragic character Kira (Emilia Clarke), the hardened pirate/thief Beckett (Woody Harrelson), the iconic Chewbacca (Joonas Suotamo), and the rogue Lando Calrissian (Donald Glover).

The story that transpires is a combination of western, swashbuckling adventure, buddy comedy, romance, and organized crime drama story. And that is where the movie is its weakest: it attempts to do so much at once, that it ends up having all of those parts together being less than what they could have been on their own. Add seeing every legendary thing that you have ever heard about Han Solo happen in the space of a two hour movie (this includes the *Millennium Falcon*, in the first example I know of a space ship having a character arc), and it certainly feels to be thinly spread.

Enter the actors to save the day. Of the main cast, there isn't a phoned in performance to be seen. These A-list celebrities certainly show why they're such beloved actors. The stand outs are Ehrenreich and Glover, both doing a surprisingly fantastic job of adhering to the mannerisms and speech patterns of the familiar Solo and Calrissian. While Ehrenreich's performance evolves to show a Solo learning to be the scoundrel that we love, Glover gives more well-deserved screen time to Calrissian with a performance so close to the original actor, Billy Dee Williams, that if one were to close their eyes they would be hard pressed to identify which one is speaking.

(Picture copyright of Lucasfilm/Walt Disney Pictures).

And, it helps, that the script dialogue doesn't feel forced or rife with unnecessary expositional dumps, but actually with people talking to one another. Apart from the earlier mentioned thinness, the writing, from page one to end, is quite good.

As for the musical score, sound effects, set design, and generally everything else, they are all quintessentially *Star*

Wars – from the sound of Han's blaster firing, to Chewbacca's roar, to the rumble of the *Falcon*'s thrusters. Fans will have plenty of meat and potato *Star Wars* to satisfy their appetite. (Except, noticeably, the iconic news-reel-like scrolling text at the beginning).

In the end, this is who this movie is directed toward: the fans of *Star Wars*. If you don't go into this movie knowing about the labyrinth of lore connected to it, then the "oohs" and "ahs" of the people around you will be quite confusing (especially during one very notable cameo, tee-hee). There is little attempt to bring new people into the fold of fandom, or to convince those on the fence about liking *Star Wars*. There were no Jar-Jar Binks-esque attempts to force a campy laugh or to cater to children in particular.

(Picture copyright of Lucasfilm/Walt Disney Pictures).

At the forefront, this movie has respect for the people who have loved this franchise and wanted to be treated to a deeper look into the lore. Sure, there will be plenty of people saying that they imagined certain events of Han Solo's past in a different way, but so would everyone. Go into this movie with the knowledge that this is *Star Wars* for *Star Wars* lovers, and maybe you too can experience what those apple cheeks and wide eyes feel like again.

Carl R. Jennings.

JURASSIC WORLD: FALLEN KINGDOM
(2018)

(Picture copyright of Amblin Entertainment).

<u>Directed by J.A. Bayona.</u>

<u>Written by Derek Connolly, Colin Trevorrow and Michael Crichton (characters).</u>

<u>Starring Chris Pratt, Bryce Dallas Howard, Rafe Spall and more.</u>

Story goes; It's been three years since the events of Jurassic World unfolded, and Owen and Claire are back with a few new friends and more dinos.

Fizzy drink bigger than my face? Check.

Nachos that will inevitably be gone before the trailers are finished? Check.

And; Action!

A fantastic start with plenty of action before the classical skeletal t-rex even appears on the title screen. The main storyline is packed with enough twists; including a very large one in relation to Mr. Lockwood's granddaughter, to keep the audience guessing, as well as enough meat in the story to keep it easy to follow. The pace of the film was neither too slow burning nor was it so fast moving that it was unintelligible - the fact that I was bursting for the toilet five minutes in and still managed to hold on until the end is paramount to that.

The introduction of new characters; some whom I genuinely ended up surprised at, as well as the inclusion and mention of more well known characters kept the film both fresh and in line with the rest of the franchise.

Beginning with a few intrepid explorers, the film soon gains traction and speeds into dinosaur action. There is a delightful balance of action, comedic moments, emotional heart tugs and scientific geekiness. I would say, however, that it focuses more on the genetics rather than the dinosaurs themselves.

(Picture copyright of Amblin Entertainment).

There is less Jeff Goldblum than I would have liked, and an appearance from the original specimen all the way from 1993!

The acting is impeccable; despite some typecasting, with both Chris Pratt and Bryce Dallas-Howard making Owen and Claire believable and endearing, with Rafe Spall, Ted Levine, BD Wong and Toby Jones playing very multi-dimensional characters.

New cast members include the fantastic 'scaredy-cat' Franklin (Justice Smith) and the more gung-ho, Zia. I would have to say that even the more senior, more experienced cast

154

were overshadowed by young Isabella Sermon, who played Maisie Lockwood. A stellar performance from such a young girl.

All in all, I would say go and see this. It is an amazing film, especially for those who have followed the franchise.

K.B. Crawford.

WILDLING (2018)

Directed by Fritz Böhm.

Written by Fritz Böhm and Florian Eder.

Starring Liv Tyler, Bel Powley, Brad Dourif and more.

(Picture copyright of Maven Pictures).

Written by first time film maker Fritz Bohm, this is a new twist on the lycanthrope legend. It begins as a very dark tale of a young girl incarcerated in a basic small room in isolation by a man she knows only as 'Daddy', her only visitor. She is not educated or allowed outside for her own protection. Daddy tells her of the dangers of the outside world, trying to scare her with fables along the lines of, 'His teeth are sharp and so are his nails. He ate all the other children. You're the last one left.'

Anna dreams of the forest outside her barred window and longs to be free but Daddy wants to keep Anna a child, however time is moving on and her mind and body are changing. When she begins to go through puberty, Daddy begins a chain of cruel events that eventually leads to Anna being rescued by Liv Tyler's character, Ellen, who takes the teenager in until a family member can be found to look after her. Ellen notices how difficult it is for her to adjust to normal life and knows some type of psychological abuse has taken place. Ellen's teenage son helps Anna to adapt, but she longs for the freedom of the forest to know more about herself rather than pander to the rules and formalities of normal life. She wanders into the forest and meets a strange man clad in animal skins who may be able to tell her more about who she really is and how she came to be.

This is a clever and sometimes unsettling story which disturbed me in parts. Dark viewing at times.

Andrea Bickerstaff.

WINCHESTER (2018)

Directed by the Spierig brothers.

Written by the Spierig brothers and Tom Vaughn.

Starring Helen Mirren, Sarah Snook, Finn Scicluna-O'Prey and more.

Set in the early twentieth century, this film tells the true story of eccentric heiress Sarah Winchester, widow of William Wirt Winchester of the Winchester Repeating Arms Company. She built a vast one hundred room mansion in San Jose with her large inheritance in order to hide away from the guilt and what she perceived to be the ghosts of the victims shot by her husband's invention. Sarah believed she had to aid the spirits to rest because a medium told her so and she also claimed a psychic connection to these apparent spirits within the house, a house which featured oddities such as stairs which led to nowhere, secret passageways and a labyrinth of hallways - all to confuse the dead!

(Copyright of Blacklab Entertainment).

Eric Price (Jason Clarke) is a psychologist sent to her home to assess her mental competence to remain a main shareholder in her husband's company and he experiences some of the mansion's ghostly resonance. He questions the reasons why the house is forever changing and why work on the rooms continues night and day. The reason for the ever changing construction is to appease the ghosts and put them to rest but this doesn't always work and some of the spirits are sealed in various rooms with thirteen nails. Sarah's niece, Marion, and her great nephew who live there also are all too well aware of her strange ways and see no problem with her behaviour having encountered some of the supernatural occurrences themselves. A particularly stubborn spirit is causing trouble for the family and must be laid to rest it seems.

Although this film hasn't received great reviews, to its credit the viewer gets to decide what is myth and what is reality. The history behind the story also intrigued me and there are some good scares in there too, even though it is not a horror in the conventional sense. After all, who can't resist a good haunted house story?

Andrea Bickerstaff.

(Copyright of Blacklab Entertainment).

TELEVISION

WESTWORLD (Season 2)

WARNING: MAJOR SPOILERS AHEAD!

(Picture copyright of HBO/Bad Robot).

Showrunner: Jonathan Nolan.

Starring Evan Rachel Wood, Thandie Newton, Jeffrey Wright, James Marsden, Ed Harris, Anthony Hopkins and more.

In my review of *Westworld*, season 1, in the debut issue of this publication, I stated that although the series was outstanding there was no need for any more seasons as the story was now told. I was very wrong indeed.

Season 2 picks up exactly where we left the action prior, with most of the robot 'Hosts' now sentient and their memories of the countless times they were murdered, raped and otherwise by the human tourists fully restored. Unsurprisingly they are out for revenge and in this most recent run, we see a lot of that realised, the quest for bloody vengeance led by nice girl turned extreme badass, Dolores Abernathy, and her beau, Teddy, who has also himself turned hardcore killer robot after Dolores meddled with his internal programming.

In other developments, we learn that former robot saloon madame, Maeve, didn't escape to the real world after all, and instead chose to remain in the ultra-violent theme park to find and rescue her daughter from another life/programmed narrative.

(Picture copyright of HBO/Bad Robot).

Other plotlines (told over multiple time frames) include more back story for William/Man in Black and his relationship with his daughter and recently deceased wife, more details about the sinister Delos company who owns the park, and an absolutely beautifully emotional explanation episode dedicated to the mysterious Native American Indian 'Ghost Nation'.

In addition, we finally get to visit some of the other theme parks, like Shogun-world and Taj-world and Anthony Hopkins' mad scientist creator, Dr. Robert Ford, also returns from the dead mid-season, in the forms of a computer programme of his consciousness (think the 'Matrix' from Classic *Doctor Who*) haunting Bernard and flashback.

This season really does go beyond everything that has come before, in a series of breathtakingly grand splendour to view on the screen and to think about for long after, posing some of the biggest philosophical questions of them all, such as the true nature of free will, existentialism and notions of a divine creator. You really do need to fully dedicate your time to each episode, with no distractions, and even then it is still quite complex with a lot to take on board. But I promise you it will be worth it.

One of the best television series' in a long time, I cannot wait for season 3 now, which has recently been confirmed.

Trevor Kennedy.

(Pictures copyright of HBO/Bad Robot).

LOST IN SPACE

Creators: Irwin Allen, Matt Sazama and Burk Sharpless.

Starring Molly Parker, Toby Stephens, Maxwell Jenkins and more.

The year was 1998 and I was immensely enjoying my

favorite show on television, *Star Trek: Voyager*. It was in its third year of production. It had so much going for it that it had me hooked from the start. The premise was a Starfleet crew had found itself stranded in the Delta Quadrant, 70,000 light years from home. It was going to take them seventy-five years to get back home to Earth at their highest warp speed. To make a long story short within the span of seven years they eventually did just that. Yet, before their run was over there was a film that made its debut in the same year. It was *Lost in Space* starring William Hurt as Professor John Robinson and Gary Oldman as the villainous Dr. Smith. This film was a remake of the campy television series that ran from 1965 to 1968. It also had distinct differences from *Voyager*. Here, as in the original, was a family set with the task of finding a new home for humanity in another star system. Something goes wrong like sabotage and they get lost in space. Unlike *Voyager*, they had no charts to help them set a course back to Earth. They were left only with the mystery of what their next adventure would be. I found that fascinating. They were truly lost without a clue as to whether their mission would succeed or not. I must have watched that film a dozen times patiently waiting for a worthy sequel. It unfortunately never came.

Then one day in the earlier part of this year I saw a trailer on YouTube about *Lost in Space* coming to Netflix as a series in April. I thought to myself it was probably just another fan made video. So, I tried to ignore it, but something said to me to just play it anyway. I did and was flabbergasted. I couldn't wait until April presented itself in the quickest fashion possible. And I must say it has not disappointed me at all. This incarnation of *Lost in Space* is also a remake, but more importantly a re-imagining of the classic 1965 version that aired on CBS. Like previous versions this one has a strong connection to literary masterpieces. The first was the novel the *Swiss Family Robinson* by Johann David Wyss (1812) and the other respectively being *Robinson Crusoe* by Daniel Defoe (1719).

When it aired in April I knew very little of what to expect

aside from what I saw on the trailer. I'm a bit of an old school kind of a person. I prefer to be surprised than to glance at the plot through countless unnecessary trailers. Yes, I could wait. So, imagine the look on my face when I clicked play and was presented with not one film, but a ten episode season! I believe my words were along the lines of - *Well damn, this is interesting*. The thing I noticed first in this version was that it depicts real world twenty-first century family life in all of its complexities. In addition to this, there is a cast that is resoundingly diverse. Yes, that's right, the Robinsons are not the only ones lost in space. There are several families stranded, again by way of sabotage on a world that at firsts appears fit for human habitation. They each have a story that surely will be told at some point, perhaps as to why they were chosen for this mission and so forth. It's just that for this introduction of *Lost in Space* the initial focus is on the Robinson's family.

(Picture copyrright of Netflix).

This Robinson family is as functional as a blood related nerd family can be. There's so much back story that accompanies them. Maureen has a biracial daughter from as of yet an unidentified black father. John is the biological father of their youngest children, Penny and Will. It has not been explained when, where, and how they met. Speaking of which, in this tale it was suggested even in the mildest of forms that if you didn't meet the criteria of a fit colonist you could quite possibly be separated from your family. How long and the ramifications of such a possibility is unknown and yet so timely during real world politics. It is revealed later on, however, that maternal instinct 'trumps' science every time. Maureen forges Will's test results enabling him to make the voyage with the rest of his family. So, with these things placed in a position to provide fans such as myself plenty of content to warrant several more seasons, it is a non-human that steals the show.

The robot says methodically 'Danger Will Robinson'. You should question the validity of this warning because the robot in this adaptation is not exactly what it seems (sorry, no big spoilers here). The two meet near a crash site surrounded by fire. They need each other to survive. Will takes the first step and befriends the robot. When attacked or the sense of danger presents itself as plausible for Will Robinson, the robot goes into attack mode. Here I found a nod to the 1998 film that the writers and producers could have possibly incorporated into the robot's back story. At some point in time in that film the mischievousness of Dr. Smith catches up with him. He soon becomes infected by a alien race of spiders that mutates his body, combining both human and alien DNA into a monstrous new being. Although hideous, the creature serves as a protector to Will Robinson replacing the need for a robot. In this Netflix version, the robot releases spider like tentacles when it's time for battle, so here it would seem that they combined these two elements - an alien spider race and the pinnacle of human artificial intelligence perhaps?

I predict that the second season will take the concept of man and machine to heights that no current show has displayed yet. Hopefully anyway, and when it is all said and done the Robinsons may no longer be lost in space after all.

Abdul-Qaadir Taariq Bakari-Muhammad.

FROSTBITE by Dave Jeffery

"A fast paced, cross-genre thriller that contains more twists and turns than a mountain road." – DARK MUSINGS

"An exciting adventure set in a bleak and dangerous landscape. The twists and turns keep on coming." - GBHBL OFFICIAL REVIEWS.

Frostbite: On this trip, it won't be the cold that kills you...

Out NOW from Severed Press and Beacon Publishing AudioBooks!

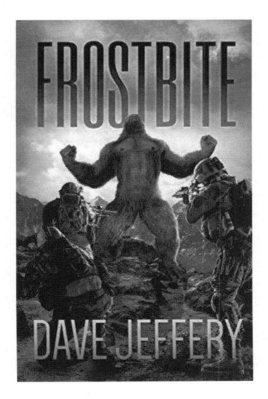

Some current titles available from Azoth Khem Publishing on Amazon....

If you would like to contact us at **Phantasmagoria Magazine** with feedback or submissions we are available through the following:

E-mail: tkboss@hotmail.com

Facebook:
https://www.facebook.com/Phantasmagoria-Magazine-322070021630736/

Twitter: @TKBossPhantasm

Back issues are still available to purchase from Amazon in print form and on Kindle and also in print form from Forbidden Planet, Belfast, and Vivo, 937 Crumlin Road, Belfast.

Phantasmagoria Magazine will return at the end of August 2018.

92685558R00092

Made in the USA
Lexington, KY
08 July 2018